The Confessions Of Church Girls

Marchet Denise Fullum

Copyright © 2016 Marchet Denise Fullum

All rights reserved.

ISBN-13: 9781519098726

DEDICATION

This book is dedicated to my family and the "FAITHFUL" few who have been with me during this entire process. Thank you for loving me, praying for me, encouraging me, and always believing that this book would become a reality! I realize how extremely BLESSED I am to have each of you and I am confident that the best is yet to come…I love you all BIG!
I also would like to thank everyone that ever tried to hinder, hurt, or hate on me! Thank you because through it all I've learned to USE IT ALL AS FUEL!

"Sometimes you just can't explain in words when you shed weights, let go of people, sort through pain, step over others' expectations, dodge drama, skip the skeptics, & begin walking towards the freedom of being who you were always intended to be! If I wasn't "rooted" I probably would have quit a long time ago but ironically enough my journey thus far has now become my fuel!"-**Marchet aka Church Girl**

For I know the plans I have for you," declares the LORD, "plans to prosper you and not to harm you, plans to give you hope and a future. – **Jeremiah 29:11**

The Confessions Of Church Girls

FOREWORD	vii
Words From My Ace	10
Introduction	12

The Foundation

God, My God, I Can't Thank You Enough	23
A Conversation Between Two Church Girls	25
Deposits	31
It's Time To Take The Hinges Off The Door	36
How Can This Be? -Church Girl Chronicles	43

The Lessons

In The Beginning Was Love	47
I Never Thought I Could Feel This Way	51
Why?	58
A Day after Independence Day	62
I Ask Myself	70
Check Your Price Tag	75

The Process

Bust The Windows Out Your Car	80
Putting Things In The Right Perspective	88
A Small Broom & Dust Pan	95
Maui	103
It Took Me A Long Time To Get These Feet Off My Neck	112
Broke Down, No Fight In Them, Hiding Behind The Curtain Believers	117

Spring Cleaning	122
Rest	126

The Purpose

Introduce Yourself…Introduce Yourself	130
It Is What It Is!	134
I've Learned Through This Process	139
Lately	142
Loving Yourself	145
Purpose	151
Marchet	158

FOREWORD

When I tell you that my sister Chet and I were raised in church, I mean that as literally as possible. Our parents had us attending church on Wednesday night, Friday night, every other Saturday morning, and all three services on Sunday. Looking back on it now, I can say it with a smile and can see the positive foundational role that time in church has played in our lives. Years later, we cannot help but mess around with our mom though and ask if we could have missed a few of the services and still loved the Lord just as much?!

While at times it makes us laugh to look back at the dizzying church attendance record, we had as a family, it also causes us to reflect on the impact it has on our perspectives and the manner in which we approach life. Our upbringing rooted us firmly in Christian family values as they were taught to us and a firm belief in the importance of our own personal relationships with God. Like the experience of many other adults that grew up in church, adulthood has provided a variety of challenges that has caused my sister to question, reflect on, and grow her own faith as she navigates this gift of life that God has blessed us all with. Knowing truths such as there is nothing too big or small for God to handle, causes introspect as we face the ups and downs of life such as the unexpected loss of a loved one or the dissolution of a relationship we thought would last forever.

This book is an intimate glance into the reckoning of Chet's own personal walk with God and the complexities of life that threatened to end that relationship rather than strengthen it. It removes the pretenses of a charmed life lived by all faithful church goers that we have the propensity to display to one another and speaks towards the need to acknowledge and address vulnerabilities in our personal faith. My sister has always had the desire to help others and has a God given gift to communicate effectively to a wide range of people. As you read the passionate words that fill the pages in this book you will see that its genesis is nested in these two core elements of her. While she has always been an eloquent speaker that excels in front of an audience, her written voice has always had the extraordinary ability to connect with a reader on a personal level in the same manner as two close friends speaking in a park.

Just like when we were kids, I have been able to avoid making certain errors that my older sister experienced for the both of us.

This book provides the same opportunity on a much larger scale to each of you that reads it. By exposing her own missteps, my sister aims to help others avoid some of the heartache she has personally experienced. While I know this collection of pieces will speak to many women, I believe it will minister to a multitude of men as well as we look to improve our own capacity to strengthen and nurture the women in our lives. Sit back and enjoy this labor of love as my sister chats with each of you as only she could.

A proud brother,

Glenn J. Butler

Words from My Ace

"Confession: acknowledgment; avowal; admission. Blogger now turned author Marchet Denise Fullum is unafraid, unmoved and unashamed to offer her confessions by opening the volumes of her past and share with you the details that have shaped her into the mighty woman she is today. She steps out in boldness to share with you some innermost thoughts and experiences that will make you laugh, cry, and sigh. A sigh of relief that you are not alone and that other church girls have been there, done that...too! More importantly, you will know that there is calm after the storm, healing after the hurt, joy after the pain, and hope in the midst of destruction and feeling downtrodden. She reminds you that no matter what you've done, there is therefore now no condemnation and that the sun will shine again! She opens her heart and her writing to women of all backgrounds, cultures, denominations, and experiences. Marchet inspires us to continue to press onward and to keep smiling! Be aware, the acknowledgments, avowals, and admissions are for all…even for those that have never stepped foot in a church. I encourage you to now step in, suspend all judgment, and focus on the life lessons and words of encouragement that will speak to you through these…The Confessions of Church Girls!"

Cassundra Ware

Aka My Ace

INTRODUCTION

Have you ever had an idea that you have been putting off for years? The one that has been on your "To Do List" and you had every intention of doing BUUUUUUUUUT years have passed by and ummmm it still isn't done. Well, I have a

CONFESSION to make…guilty!

GUILTY...GUILTY...GUILTY of not setting aside time to pursue one of my passions...writing! So now in 2016 I finally sat my chocolate self-down to complete one of many to come. I set time aside to jot down my thoughts that had been scribbled in journals, jotted down on Post-It Notes, and typed in files throughout my computer for years. It is my opportunity to release what's been stored in my mind and unveil what has been on my heart in phase one of "The Confessions of Church Girls."

I never imagined that as I was finally about to publish this book that my life would be where it is now. For a while now I think I have been intentionally putting off the publishing of this book because I knew that within these pages lied the potential to set so many other people free. To some that may initially seem like all the motivation one would need to go ahead and complete this book. However, for me I realized the responsibility that lies with publishing this book and at the same time my everyday real life was still in progress. There were many days that I was just emotionally empty and physically drained. Over the past 7 years or so my life seemed to be crumbling apart. Every time I uttered "I don't think I can hurt more than this!" MORE showed up! There were many days I just didn't feel like it any more. A part of me was embarrassed because I'm usually the one cheering everyone else on but I found myself realizing I needed encouragement too!

For a while now I've known that this was something that I was supposed to be doing...writing. In fact, at a young age my Pastor, Dr. Wayne E. Anderson, spoke prophetically over my life one night during a church service. He said, "Now Marchet I see you working with and sitting in front of computers." Let me pause really quick and interject that this was waaaaayyyyy before Apple or Microsoft was as big as they are today. In fact, back then when people said the word "apple" you immediately thought of a piece of fruit and not a light weight laptop or iPhone. That may be hard for some of you younger folks to believe but it's indeed a fact. Now, let's go back to that night. In that moment when Pastor Anderson was speaking to me, I remember thinking the person before me was going to be a doctor, and the person before that was going to preach the gospel, and you see me working with computers?!? Really? LOL!!! Pastor Anderson must have been able to not just hear from God but to also hear what I was just thinking. He then said to me, "If you can only see what I can see. You are going to be sooooo blessed!"

At that moment I must CONFESS I didn't see it but now almost 30 years later…as I have spent many late night and early mornings "in front of my "Apple" computer I chuckle realizing this is what Pastor Anderson was trying to get me to see! He was planting a seed that popped up many times as I was writing this book. There have been many days where I wanted to doubt that this was something I was supposed to be doing because I have always been a little different. What if the church folks kick me out? What if my friends who aren't Christians think I'm a weirdo? What if no one buys it? What if...? What if...? What if...? I'm telling you I almost literally drowned in the oasis of "what ifs." In fact, I almost allowed my "what ifs" to take my purpose under completely.

On top of my "what ifs" there was so much going on in my life that I continued to allow circumstances, situations, the past, emotions, problems, doubts, and my fears to cloud my vision. Instead of pressing forward, I found myself constantly going in circles. The same tears, mess, circumstances, choices, need for growth, and an increase in faith made my journey a pitiful one. The same sad tune always decorated my stagnate life. The same excuses and complaints abided in my conversations on a regular basis. Until, one night when the tears rolled once again because I had allowed my priorities to get jumbled up. Instead of grabbing for the Kleenex, the phone, or a pillow to drown my pitiful face in. I grabbed my laptop. I realized that my victory was going to come through me ministering to others through writing. There's definitely an enemy tugging on every weak area of my life trying to keep me from aligning myself in line with what I know I'm supposed to be doing. It's one thing to know what you're supposed to be doing but if you never just go ahead and do it you won't conquer your fears or touch the lives of others.

I had to learn how to navigate through difficult situations as a "shift" in my marital life and a "shift" in my circle of friends was occurring right before my eyes. As others looked in, they were oftentimes fooled by the appearance of people around me but the reality of the matter is the FAITHFUL few began to identify themselves and the numbers had drastically declined. Many assumed my phone was always ringing, my home was always filled with those who were genuine, and my schedule never had openings. The reality of the matter is my phone actually ringing for me was a rare occurrence, my home hardly ever had anyone else in it but my two daughters and I, and my schedule (though it was full) was hardly ever about me. My life though busy was filled with church responsibilities, my daughter's activities, single mother life accountabilities, and those who saw me as their 911 dumpster (oops I mean operator…SMILE).

Sometimes throughout our lives our purpose is manifesting itself in various areas of our lives. For me it always amazed me how so many women, when I was in college, would pop into my dorm apartment and pour out their hearts. Or in general how many women enjoyed telling me their men stories, their victories, their upbringing, or their broken heart stories. It seems like every time I turned around someone had something else to tell me. I finally realized that I needed to put what I've experienced in a book and to take the time out to type out what God has given me so it could bless a wide range of women. I also believe that it will reach and cause thought provoking conversation amongst so many men.

What I know for sure is if I would have published this book about 7 years ago it would have lacked the wisdom and life lessons I have gained. I was still angry then and even though anger does sometimes make for great fuel when writing. I didn't want the entire book to just be confessions of an ANGRY CHOCOLATE WOMAN. I needed to realize that my daughters would read this book, my family, my friends, my church family, my haters, my co-workers, nosey folks, critical people, and anyone else who purchased it. For a moment I think that added to the delay of publishing this book but then I ran across a quote from Anne Lamont that said:

"You own everything that happened to you. Tell your stories. If people wanted you to write warmly about them, they should have behaved better."

After reading this it was as if the weight of the matter was lifted off of me and I realized "it is what it is!" Some may disagree, some may not understand, some may be encouraged, some may be angered, some may be challenged to take an inventory of their lives so they can make some adjustments, and some may see themselves right within these pages. Whatever the case maybe I would be a bold face liar if I CONFESSED to all of you that this entire process has been a vivid colorful picture of me dancing through purple and yellow flowers with not a care in the world. In these pages lies my stories thus far. Some are funny and some are very hurtful. I have lived the realities of these pages and I am better because of it all. Though I wanted to quit many times I kept pressing on and I know that has to do with the prayers of people that took the time to pray for me. As well as, the FAITHFUL few I have in my life who wouldn't allow me to quit. My prayer today is that whoever reads this book "The Confessions Of Church Girls" gets something from it and your eyes are opened just a little bit more.

The title alone will cause many to speculate or immediately think they know what to expect already. However, I will just say "YOU THINK YOU KNOW BUT YOU HAVE NO IDEA!" The best part about this book is that I have FREED myself from feeling that this has to be anything more than GENUINE! There is no perfect formula other than ensuring every time my fingertips hit the keys of my keyboard that I don't hold back but I deliver! I do have to warn you that I'm one of those writers who probably breaks a lot of grammatical rules. When I write I find myself engaged in the moment with no literal concern for what others think. It's oftentimes is my personal therapy session where I'm sifting through my current circumstances & sincerely articulating my feelings. I'm telling you this in advance so that those of you that are not use to reading from a writer that admittedly breaks grammatical rules can prepare yourself for my world of writing. It definitely is not my intent for my writing to be a distraction but a blessing to your life.

So WELCOME to these sessions of CONFESSIONS and to this time of RELEASE! Most importantly to this vision being put into action right in front of your eyes. I personally want to thank so many of you that encouraged me along the way. I'm sure for some of you I have sounded like the little boy that cried wolf because I have talked about publishing this book for years now. I had to finally get over the fear of what people may think and remember that my true heart behind this entire process has always been if I could just save one person from experiencing some of the heart wrenching things, I have experienced it will be well worth it!

So, as you read this book allow yourself to digest the truths and the transparent realities that I am going to share about my life. I don't hold any titles. I don't profess to know it all. I don't have an extensive education in theology. However, what I do have is the ability to share in my own unique way. I'm not afraid to be transparent and I get joy just thinking about the power that lies in just being authentically real! If you are reading this book now, I believe it's for a purpose. I don't expect everyone's reading experience to be the same but I do expect God to get the glory out of this entire process. For I am a living breathing witness that within us is the power to be better as we deal with ourselves! I have confidence that you'll be blessed, healed, restored, and revived. This book is an unfiltered telescope into my life and I dedicate this book to everyone that has or has not realized that they are BLESSED with PURPOSE!

Enjoy every single second…

I love you Big,

Marchet aka Church Girl

I can do all things through Christ who strengthens me. – **Philippians 4:13**

God is not a man, that he should lie; neither the son of man, that he should repent: hath he said, and shall he not do it? or hath he spoken, and shall he not make it good? **-Numbers 23:19**

THE FOUNDATION

God, My God, I Can't Thank You Enough

Psalms 30 The Message

A David Psalm

1 I give you all the credit, God— you got me out of that mess,

   you didn't let my foes gloat.

2-3 God, my God, I yelled for help

   and you put me together.

 God, you pulled me out of the grave,

   gave me another chance at life

   when I was down-and-out.

4-5 All you saints! Sing your hearts out to God!

>
> Thank him to his face!
>
> He gets angry once in a while, but across
>
> > a lifetime there is only love.
>
> The nights of crying your eyes out
>
> > give way to days of laughter.
>
> **6-7** When things were going great
>
> > I crowed, "I've got it made.
>
> I'm God's favorite.
>
> > He made me king of the mountain."
>
> Then you looked the other way
>
> > and I fell to pieces.
>
>
> **8-10** I called out to you, God;
>
> > I laid my case before you:
>
> "Can you sell me for a profit when I'm dead?
>
> > auction me off at a cemetery yard sale?
>
> When I'm 'dust to dust' my songs
>
> > and stories of you won't sell.
>
> So, listen! and be kind!
>
> > Help me out of this!"

11-12 You did it: you changed wild lament

   into whirling dance;

You ripped off my black mourning band

   and decked me with wildflowers.

I'm about to burst with song;

  I can't keep quiet about you.

God, my God, I can't thank you enough.

A Conversation Between Two Church Girls

(*For the purpose of this book I am eliminating the actual name of the other Church Girl and will refer to her as Church Girl Hawaii. I have not altered or grammatically corrected her initial writing to me intentionally.)

Church Girl Hawaii: "So I don't know if you read your messages but I needed to drunk text/write someone about this crazy mess... maybe you can help. I'm sorry if this worries you in anyway or is inconvenient but I just want to put it down and out there to anyone really. So at least one person would know and help me sort all this out. Anyway, I still have not been to church, at least since this year started. I don't care. What I do know about it is how my whole life has been governed by it, and still finds its way to screw me up even more. I don't think it's fair I have to f****n be the one to do the right thing. Don't get me wrong I prefer it just wish it was expected of me. I have serious control issues, it works into my perfectionist mentality quite well, but I think I got the negative end of the stick. Control turns more destructive rather than constructive and all my feelings point inward. I'm pretty empathetic, to a ridiculous degree, I feel what you feel, but I prefer to feel nothing or at least have the appearance of doing so. And all this mixing of feelings and numbness equal something I've got in abundance...pain. Physical mental emotional it's all there. And what ends the pain? I do. Nothing does. And in case you can't make the correlation I am nothing. Therefore, nothing is wrong with me. And nothing couldn't be any better. But I hate it (again with the control thing). I hate hate hate hate hate it...me. Wrote it into my arm to prove it. I get to see hate's shining face every day forever. God, I really wish you were here. Even though you'd probably pray and I'd be really annoyed for a while but continue to talk to you anyway. I think...well thinking is pretty much what got me her in the first place. Always thinking. I think if I thought a little less my life would be easier, more proactive. I'd be out there drunk with company, probably getting laid. But thinking brought me here, alone drunk and bleeding. I had it all set up. Was set to have a good time by the worlds standards but I couldn't do it. I don't know why. Just couldn't do it. So, I came back home and drank despite myself...or maybe to spite myself. Cut open this flesh of mine and started to write. Figures I talked to the chaplain earlier about my problems. Turns out it's not so uncommon, not a red flag at all and there are plenty of places I can turn to for help. F**k him. He doesn't know me, doesn't have any clue how to correct me judge me fix me. I tried I really did to help him see me, but he just wasn't focused enough. I cried for help in the only way I knew and he didn't know so f**k it. I don't need help. I need grey goose...and weed...and a f****n skateboard. Then I can die happy. And that doesn't sound so bad. I'm going to knock out now...will continue soon."

MY RESPONSE:

"1st let me say I LOVE YOU! I'm not sure how much weight that carries for the words you so honestly wrote I have literally written and felt them all before. In fact, I have been doing A WHOLE LOT of writing over the past month. All of a sudden, I pick up my computer and I let it all out. I, yes, "I" am even seeing the Chaplin once a week right here in Italy. This chocolate church girl wanted to let you know that I acknowledge, recognize, and know what you are feeling is real. I am glad that you are letting it out. What I have found is that most "church girls" don't let it out and just like in the natural constipation is never good. It hurts often when it comes out. It takes work to get it out. But the key is to get it out. Can I say one more time that I LOVE YOU Church Girl Hawaii. I love you because whether you acknowledge it or not there is a survivor in you. There is a wanting to be so uniquely pure that you won't settle to be the "cookie cut Christian." There is nothing wrong with that. What we don't have enough of is "REAL church girls" to tell you it's o.k. To tell you that you are right on the money but that no amount of alcohol, weed, or a cool relaxing yet invigorating ride on a skateboard will deal with what we have to deal with ourselves. If I told you that the process was going to be a "Disney world" ride of your lifetime I would be lying. What I can tell you is that for once in my life at I finally took the time to be REAL with myself. Just like you I reached out to the one person I thought could take my occasional cuss words, anger, and frustration. For I knew underneath it all was a young "church girl' hurting but full of purpose. You have to understand and accept that your purpose maybe unique and never seen yet within or outside the Christian church walls. What I'm learning is it's not other people that we necessarily fear not being accepted from but it in fact is our own inner war that keeps us hostage to the years of stuff that has piled in our heart, soul, and mind. What I know for sure is that you will be just fine...why because you have me to be that bouncing board, the one to be honest, give you some answers, but yet give you the space to be yourself...with no judgment. I pray you don't have a bad hangover and that when you read the words, I am typing you will feel that I am no different from you...because I'm too a "church girl" working through my own issues. I end the same way I started. I LOVE YOU Church Girl Hawaii!!"

I received the above email when I was going through some very difficult times myself. I vowed to myself to include this in my first book. It shows that there are real live church girls that are dealing with real life things. Church girls that were raised in church and you would think we would be able to recite every answer and avoid some oftentimes obvious pitfalls. The reality of the matter is that we don't.

I started to realize that we weren't releasing enough yet we had become church girls that suppress and move on. I've often said what we don't deal with now we will eventually have to deal with it later. We can no longer be well programed robots but we have to deal with what's dealing with us. There are many hurting church girls that are just like Church Girl Hawaii. They are fighting to love themselves and to feel comfortable in just being. They love God but they have suppressed issues that are no longer staying tucked in. If that is you today, I want you to know that you are not alone. I want you to know that it's ok to deal with it. You can free yourself from the criticism and judgments of others. While allowing yourself to sort through your life up to this point. You don't have to be afraid and you don't have to put if off another day. You can freely release and trust me it will be well worth it.

Have I not commanded you? Be strong and courageous. Do not be frightened, and do not be dismayed, for the LORD your God is with you wherever you go.
Joshua 1:9

Deposits

Earlier this year I told both my daughters that I needed to have a conversation with them. As odd as this may seem they both were SUPER excited because they actually like talking to me. As we met at the dining room table their little legs were swinging from their chairs and their faces were decorated with smiles as they waited for their Mommy to start the conversation.

I started off by telling them that I LOVE them both BIG and that I was really proud of how they have handled our entire transition process. It was important for me to make sure that they knew I understood many of the sacrifices they had to make and that I appreciated them for being troopers throughout it all.

I then went on to tell them that it was time for us to start making DEPOSITS into their savings accounts. I wanted them to know that the money they get right now I want them to tithe, give an offering, and then save the rest. Everything they needed & some of their wants I would take care of so there was no reason why they could not make consistent DEPOSITS into their savings accounts.

So, I then went on to tell them Mommy is going to take you to the bank and each of you are going to open your own accounts. You are going to walk in with your heads held high, smiles on your faces, and money in your purses. I said Mommy is going to practice with you now so you will be confident on that day! Most of the people you may deal with will be older, taller, and adults....so Mommy wants you to look them in the eye which is called "eye contact" and firmly reach your hand out to shake their hand as they approach you. I then reassured them that it would be okay and that it was absolutely normal to feel a little nervous. Just know Mommy will be right there to coach you (if you need it) along the way.

Then I arranged the table to look like the desk they would be led to at the bank. We went through each scenario that could come up and practiced the whole routine. I wanted to make sure that Jayda Louise Fullum and Anzel Marchet Fullum understood what they were about to do. As well as, understood the importance of making regular DEPOSITS. I will never forget how proud I was when we really went to the bank and how empowered they both were!!! It was because I took the time to make DEPOSITS in their lives that they now knew the power and significance of regular DEPOSITS!

This morning that entire experience came to mind as I opened my Facebook account and received such a thoughtful post on my wall it read:

"MAY YOU ALWAYS BE BLESSED WITH WALLS FOR THE WIND.

A ROOF FOR THE RAIN.

A WARM CUP OF TEA BY THE FIRE.

LAUGHTER THAT CHEERS YOU.

THOSE YOU LOVE NEAR YOU.

AND ALL THAT YOUR HEART MAY DESIRE."-IRISH BLESSING

I immediately thought what a wonderful DEPOSIT! Then my mind began to click, as it often does, and I knew it was time to write this down for this book. I just want to encourage all of you reading this that there is SO MUCH POWER IN MAKING DEPOSITS INTO OTHERS! I know it's easy to get caught up in ourselves, or in our circumstances, or in our to-do-list, or within our four walls but wouldn't it be a nice change of pace if each of us PURPOSELY MADE REGULAR DEPOSITS into the life of someone else. I can't even full articulate how the DEPOSIT on my Facebook page impacted me but I will say this it meant more to me because I didn't even expect it. It wasn't done because I had talked to her recently in fact I haven't talked to her face to face since earlier in 2012 when I lived in Italy. It meant so much because it was a JUST BECAUSE DEPOSIT with no strings attached!

My challenge to each of you that is reading this book is to begin to make more intentional thought-out DEPOSITS into other people's lives. The possibilities are limitless and way bigger than just Facebook or this actual book. What I know for sure is our lives begin to be a little sweeter when we DEPOSIT into the life of someone else! DO IT and watch how POWERFUL your DEPOSITS become! It's not deep it's just SO ESSENTIAL and NEEDED in so many people's lives! You may be the first person that has actually took the time to DEPOSIT in their lives or your DEPOSITS can eliminate a negative balance in their lives! Don't hesitate, don't over think it, but allow your life to become a movement towards daily finding opportunities to DEPOSIT in the lives of others! You cannot go wrong when you live a life that is beyond DEPOSITING to just yourself. DEPOSIT! DEPOSIT!

DEPOSIT! while you have the opportunity too! Tomorrow is not promised!

And we know that in all things God works for the good of those who love him, who have been called according to his purpose. - **Romans 8:28**

It's Time to Take the Hinges Off the Door

A couple of days ago my "**ACE**" Cassundra came over after work. I was in my room a little frustrated about my closet doors because they constantly get off track. Even when both doors are on correctly it's hard for me to fully see all the things that are in my closet. So of course, Case my "**ACE**" came to the rescue. She began to pull, lean, lift, and tilt each door in a sincere determination to get the doors back on track for me.

At a certain point I felt compelled to give a hand (side note there are many things I am talented at…however fixing doors and putting these closet doors back in correctly is not one of my talents LOL) since I had just been standing there looking at Casey wrestle with these doors. Finally, as we both had been pulling, leaning, lifting and tilting I said "Oh forget it just take both the doors off." Casey then replied, "Huh…are you sure?" I'm sure she was thinking this doesn't quite make sense to me right now especially since a good 20 minutes of faithful attempts to get these doors on had occurred. Yet, she willingly began to pull, lean, lift, and tilt both doors off.

Immediately after the doors came off my mind said "Hmmmm isn't it time to take the doors off the hinges?" I stood there and had a moment that usually happens before I begin to write or blog. I stood there…now in front of my closet that I could see completely in. There was **NO** section that was hidden from the doors not opening up quite enough. I no longer felt frustrated or blocked out…. what I felt was a big sense of relief. I thought man I should have done this a long time ago.

So, what does this have to do with us personally. Good question…LOL! Like my closet there is so many stories that go into how things got in there, why or where they were purchased, and really the closet ultimately tells a lot about who I am. That is like our lives! I thought how powerful it really would be if people began to take the door off the hinges of their lives. We each have a story but often times our story is hidden to the world or only portions are visible to see or grab a hold to. These doors are blocking people out.

On this day I declare that it's time to take the doors off the hinges of our lives! The first person that it will affect will be you! Although Casey was in the room when we took the doors off my closet. She wasn't quite as excited as I was because it didn't have complete meaning to her yet. She didn't know how long the doors had been off track or how long I had been frustrated with not being able to fully dig into my closet like I wanted to. In fact, she initially probably was only thrilled for me because I genuinely was excited. From her view point there were two long doors that were taller than both of us leaning against my bed and blocking some main areas in my room…lol.

I know my mind works a little different than most people but there is a wonderful parallel from this all. It wasn't until after I explained to her the story about my struggle with my closet doors…that she understood why this was so important to me. It so easy some times to prejudge people (**I CONFESS** I'm definitely guilty of this) and formulate our opinion of them because we are standing there looking at them with the doors still on the hinges. We are basically playing a guessing game because the REAL truth won't reveal itself until the doors are opened or better yet just completely off the hinges.

How much better would life be if we learn to have conversations and relationships that are foundationally based on **TRUTH**! When the doors were still on my closet, I could have told you there was some red bottom shoes in there and Boris Kodjoe would hand me clothes in the morning as he sang "You are so beautiful to me" …LOL! However, we all know (or at least you should know) if our lives became lives that had no barriers to them. Now I know someone may go really deep and say we can't be open about everything and my answer would be it all depends on how healed and open you want to be. This will always determine your end result.

I

have learned that there was so many people thinking they knew my story that it became so liberating to just tell my story myself. I promise you there were periods even recently where I wanted to make a bunch of t-shirts for me to wear that declared "**YOU THINK YOU KNOW BUT YOU HAVE NO IDEA!**" Not only did it make me chuckle sometimes but it gave me permission to not feel as if I needed to "act" or "be" anything else but my true authentic self.

Hey, I do realize this life we live is a process but one of my sisters, friends, and life coach, Shelia Lewis, always tells me "Marchet, I am going to give you the answers to this part of life so you don't have to fail the test like I did!" I love and appreciate her soooooo much for that because it taught me many valuable lessons. First of all, we don't have to remain a prisoner of our past mistakes. In fact, when you take the door off the hinges you are declaring out loud that you are not a prisoner to your past but indeed a **WORK IN PROGRESS**!

You are declaring and realizing that by taking the door off the hinges you are actually extending your hand to someone else and saying out loud "I've been there and you too **CAN** and **WILL** get through this!" You are allowing yourself to breathe again without endlessly holding your head under a sea of guilt. You will no longer continue to feel as if you have been swimming in the deep holding your breath but you can come up for air!!! You will finally be able to declare.... I Can Breathe!

Taking the hinges off the door doesn't always have to be revealing the bad in our lives there are many of us who made a lot of GREAT moves and steps in our lives.
We **conquered fears, jumped over obstacles, and avoided nonsense** and that too **NEEDS TO BE SHARED**!

The point is let's begin to be **OPEN** to the possibilities of us living **AUTHENTIC** lives! LET US be more eager to learn from each other than quick to tear one another down. **LET US** realize that once you **TAKE THE DOOR OF THE HINGES** you are opening up the pages of your life that make you who you really are…<u>and no matter what anyone else may have told you I want to reassure you that is a **WONDERFUL** thing!</u>

TAKE THE DOOR OFF THE HINGES as you see fit and I'm sure you will realize and stumble across things even you may have forgotten. What you won't be able to hide is the fabric of your life that has made you into a **MAGNIFICENT WORK**! Even if you don't see it, I declare it to be so!!! May the pages in this book be a living example of what "taking the door off the hinges" actually looks like. May this book demonstrate a life that is transparent so that you will have some cliff notes on some of the realities that can occur in life. Most importantly may you look at your life and discover that your transparency is necessary for not only yourself but someone else. Live your best life transparently covered in truth!

For God gave us a spirit not of fear but of power and love and self-control. – **2 Timothy 1:7**

How Can This Be?-Church Girl Chronicles

Have you ever found yourself living against the odds? You should have been broken? You should have been destroyed? You could have been homeless? Your bills shouldn't be getting paid? Your tears should still be flowing? You should be in a fetal position feeling extremely depressed, lonely, and forsaken? YET...YOU ARE 36,966 miles above ground level, bills paid, drinking hot tea & reflecting on your life up to this point!

For some you may have found yourself yelling at the computer screen as you declared "I was with you Marchet until you got to the YOU ARE 36,966 miles above ground level.... I'm still in Hawaii, Philadelphia, Washington, Texas, Maryland, Italy, Mississippi, Virginia, Alabama, at home, or at work" ...LOL!!!!

I was given the unique time to get away for a week. It gave me the opportunity to reflect, to regroup, and to refocus! I'm in awe of God and in awe of how everything worked out! For the entire week I would pick up my Blogger App to write but would quickly put it down because for once I NEEDED to just BE. If we're not careful we will SPRINT through life and almost make ourselves feel guilty when we take "ME" time! So, I put the app down and I was actually really proud of myself.

Ironically enough I returned to my birth state of Mississippi. The place where my wonderful mom, in 1974, gave birth to her very unique child. This trip was very much different than many of my previous trips. There were no lights, glam, men, excessive alcohol consumption, or late-night shenanigans. I actually was proud of myself that I had GROWN UP and there actually came a time in my life where my PRIORITIES CHANGED.

This CHURCH GIRL hasn't always looked forward to the PEACEFUL RETREATS that this country trip brought. Yet, I knew that to get different results in my life it was more than necessary for me to begin to do things differently. Even as I was 36,966 miles above land, I couldn't deny the fact that it was but by the GRACE OF GOD that I am still here!!! I'm accepting the fact that though many may be critical of my choice to write about the realities of being a CHURCH GIRL! I have to continue creating this platform REGARDLESS!!!

This COULD BE because I've chosen to explore and expose what may be crippling so many CHURCH GIRLS around the world. The reality of the matter is that too many of us are in denial about what's really going on! When we hold our stories in and allow traditions, fears, others' opinions, and life itself to keep us bound, defeated, and acting out based on UNREVEALED AND NON-DEALT with CHURCH GIRL experiences. Then we are PREVENTING OURSELVES from the "WHAT SHOULD BE" chapters of our lives.

I personally know too many CHURCH GIRLS who beyond the MAC Makeup, the clothes they wear, the lives they live, and often their smile lies VAULTS of UNREVEALED AND UNDEALT with CHURCH GIRL experiences! I also acknowledge that some of you can't get away to a week-long country retreat. So, I just wanted to pause and say I've been there! One of my prayers is that this book will allow many of you to escape for a moment. To remind you that there are chapters within you beyond right now!

How can this be? This can be because despite what your CHURCH GIRL experiences may or may not have been there is an UNDENIABLE TRUTH that WILL ALWAYS REMAIN God LOVES YOU!!! God has an AWESOME plan for your life and though we can't always see it I'm here to remind you GOD DOESN'T LIE! There is soooooo much POWER in your STORY! The very fact that you are still here despite it all gives me the PUSH to keep POURING OUT!

So, take a sip and let it digest! Then take this time to remind yourself that THIS TIME NEXT YEAR YOU WON'T BE IN THE SAME SPOT!

Trust in the LORD with all your heart and lean not on your own understanding- **Proverbs 3:5**

THE LESSONS

In The Beginning Was Love

The respect my husband had for me before he said I do. The same respect that led him propose to me because he was in love. In love with this chocolate sister who was different from him. He admired the hard work it took for me to complete my college education. He could see the quality of my 2-bedroom apartment that only I dwelled in. He met my family and had a pow wow with my step-father and brother. He knew that I only wanted to be married once. He knew that once I said "I do" that I meant it until the day I died.

As I think back to that time where we would share Chinese food together and eat grill cheese sandwiches from the Air Force Airmen's cafeteria. Not one day went by since the first day we met that we weren't in each other's presence. Not because we had to be but because we both couldn't think of anywhere else, we wanted to be outside of being together. I remember how I was enough and the insecurity I feel now I never felt when we were dating and then engaged.

I remember how soft his touch was as we would share a shower together. I remeber how it was a "sin" in his eyes to not softly kiss me as I entered or left his presence. I remember the way his eyes looked and how eye contact was never forced. I remember the "just because" flowers, cards, and gifts but beyond all that I remember how his love cocooned me and made me feel safe. I remember how money was never an issue because my Airmen and I had plans beyond our humble beginnings. We talked about children, traveling the world, winning the lottery, and one day owning our own home.

The key is we used to talk. I knew the words that were coming out of my mouth were hitting ears that sincerely wanted to listen. I could undress my past and invite him into my future with no hesitation. We shared everything from our childhood all the way up to the day we met. I felt as if my KING had finally arrived and I was so ready to be his Queen. I felt FREE to be myself and FREE to open up about all my fears, dreams, disappointments, and desires. I

FREELY gave myself to a man 7 years younger than me. I didn't rob the cradle he came running out and I believed Aaliyah when she sang "Age Aint Nothing but A Number."

Even today as I think about those earlier days I smile and then I shake my head in confusion not quite sure who stole "my cookie from the cookie jar." Then I get pissed because I'm not sure if it was stolen or just given away! I guess I will never really know every detail that contributed to the unraveling of our marriage. I guess I will never know how it is easier to be intimate with someone outside of your covenant vows vs. the woman you promised to love, cherish, and do no harm to. I guess I will never know why my days are filled with less emotion and my lips have not felt a kiss from my king for longer than I can remember. I guess although I didn't take my life and throw it in the air allowing pieces of it to be scattered everywhere…I am still at the end tasked at putting it all back together again.

As I watched him daily go through his routine. A routine similar to that of a black widow…I watched him intricately create a web of isolation. A web so fragile yet clear to the eye that I am in awe of the fact that he had the energy to create it. I saw him with resentment in his eyes and I know that if he didn't make a decision that I...yes, I will have to find the strength to make one. He said he was depressed and I could never really understand if that was because he felt guilty or because he missed his concubine.

Beyond him I felt like the hourglass of my life had been cheated and I grasped for the falling grains that are swarming constantly around me. I saw him exit and enter the doors of our house halfway saying goodbye or hello and I wondered what had I done to him? The answer is I don't stand here guiltless like the perfect wife who has never had a bad wife day. However, I do STAND here, as someone who has never stepped out of our marriage and for 3 consistent times has not stepped away from him as he stepped out on me. This sounds crazy I told myself the answer was to leave...but was that the answer? So, I endured more than my mind could comprehend as I continued to wrestle with divorcing him...my husband. I continue to ask myself..." In the beginning was LOVE? Right???

> But they who wait for the LORD shall renew their strength; they shall mount up with wings like eagles; they shall run and not be

weary; they shall walk and not faint. – **Isaiah 40:31**

I Never Thought I Could Feel This Way

I never thought I would feel the way I feel now. I never thought I would cry the tears I have cried. I never thought I would be in a foreign country lonely and very much alone. However, the reality is I AM. I AM hurting and although my last name is Fullum…my husband could care less. In fact, not only could he care less but he also has betrayed me in the worst way possible. Instead of being a way for a year serving our country he was a way for a year serving another woman. As I replay the phone calls, the letters, and the emails he so timely sent you would have never known that he was pleasing his wife from a distant and intimately pleasing his floozy while in Korea. I knew my husband was a talented man but I never knew the full extent of his hidden talents. He out acted some of the best of them like Denzel Washington and Tom

Cruise. He had me believing the lies that he was planting every single day he was gone. He had it mapped out like a well-planned crime scene. Both of his wife and his willing participating side piece were on his daily well-spaced-out schedule.

What I couldn't erase in my head was the pages upon pages of emails that I read containing graphic and nude pictures that "she" sent my husband. She obviously never really thought that I would see them or maybe just maybe she didn't care either way. I guess the kicker part for me is she knew he was married but in the day and time we live in now that doesn't mean anything. Especially if the man, my husband, is telling her he's getting a divorce during one or many of their adulterous sessions. I was not in covenant relationship with her so I quickly began to lower the expectations I had created as a common woman to woman code. You know the code that usually obligates you "to close your legs to married men!" That code that would cause most women to walk away and not send graphic nude pictures to another woman's husband while serving our country.

That "code" was definitely broken as I saw the picture of her, the Airmen, spread eagle. My mind couldn't help but to immediately think about the many cold nights I laid by myself. I thought about the many times my husband told me I was fat and yet endlessly accused me of cheating. My husband was making all these cheating allegations when all along he had been cheating and continued to cheat. See this wasn't the first time we were in this space called adultery. We had been in this same spot 2 other times. It was the same scenario but the previous scenarios were with different women. However, this 3rd time left me feeling stupid, vulnerable, ashamed, isolated, victimized, shameful, angry, pissed, calm, and emotionally drained all at the same time.

Now that this was the 3rd time my stomach couldn't digest the deceit and my heart couldn't contain the venomous lies that Mr. Fullum had told. Just weeks before he left for Korea, obviously to clear his own conscious, he presented me with an upgraded wedding ring. This upgraded ring was accompanied by sweet and loving words. As well as, what I thought at the time to be a beautiful, sincere, and loving letter. My husband, at the time, was constantly reassuring me that there was no other woman he wanted to spend the rest of his life with but me. He kept telling me that he was sacrificing this year away from his family so we could go as a family to Italy. For Italy was on his dream list of places to be stationed at in the Air Force. The initial pure purpose of that year in Korea quickly turned into sexual escapades with another woman. His life in Korea was different than the realities he fed myself and his two daughters over the phone and in his letters. Yet, the pain and hurtful realities of those sexual escapades would not be revealed in its entirety until we all arrived to Italy.

Prior to that I knew something was not right because MY husband after being gone for a year didn't even remember that he was the one that bought me the lingerie I slipped into on his first night back. For I had made up my mind that things would be different…that Italy would be a new chapter in our lives. Plus, at this time I didn't know about the female floozy that knew about me. So, in my head I was still eating off of all the things my husband told me on the phone, in his emails, and in the letters…that he loved me and wanted to spend the rest of his life with me. So why wouldn't I think that MY husband wouldn't start a fresh right here in Hawaii before we boarded our flights in the morning headed to California and Italy.

Little did I know that the pain I felt that night would be the springboard to all the pain that lied ahead. I would experience more pain and disappointment in just 2 weeks than I had experienced in my entire life. I would continue to lie in bed by myself, lonely, hurting, betrayed, disappointed, and literally feeling as if the wind had been knocked out of me. I often had to grab my laptop instead of grabbing a knife. I often had to grab my laptop instead of medicating myself to a numb existence. I often had to grab my laptop because if anything comes out of THIS. THIS PAIN I FEEL RIGHT NOW…THIS UNEXPLAINABLE SORROW THAT IS LINGERING OVER MY MIND AND PENETRATING MY SLEEP! IF ANYTHING COMES OUT OF THIS TENSION THAT HAS INVADED MY BACK AND THIS STRESS THAT WEIGHS HEAVILY

UPON MY SHOULDERS. IF ANYTHING COMES OUT OF THIS…I'm praying that someone else will have enough wisdom to see the signs I ignored for too long! That they will read this book and realize that someone else has felt the pain they may be feeling right now. That you do not have to stay married to someone that consistently violates the covenant of your marriage with adultery. You just have to get to a point where you are ready to deal with it and you no longer avoid what is often hurtful and humiliating. I never in a million years thought I would hurt so bad or be angry enough (with my husband who started off as a friend) to even consider wanting to hurt him physically as much as he hurt me. I also never thought my husband would cheat on me multiple times and allow his side pieces to feel worthy enough to address me. This book is my honest recollection of events that at the time I never thought I would live through. Recollections of pain remembered and typed out within the pages of these books with the intent to let someone else know your story doesn't have to end after adultery and betrayal. You can and you will pick yourself up and use it like fuel. It is absolutely endless where your past hurts can take you if you decide to

LIVE AGAIN!

God is our refuge and strength, an ever-present help in trouble. –
Psalm 46:1

Why?

I'm sitting here once again watching the DVD "Making Marriage Work" alone…should I be surprised…No I finally say to myself maybe I am lying to myself and not accepting the obvious. The obvious is that he doesn't want this marriage to work. The obvious is if I didn't find out about the other woman then they would still be secretly talking to each other today. I would just be here…here for what? I'm here because he doesn't want to lose his girls. It has absolutely nothing to do with me or with how I feel. I guess it's like seeing a killer in a room coming straight at you…or a bullet headed straight for your heart. You see it but it's so quick and catches you off guard to the point that you don't have time to respond.

If you would have told me 11 years ago that I would tolerate how I am being treated I would have laughed in your face. The truth is I have lost myself. I have lost Marchet Denise Fullum and no matter how hard I try to regain myself I am overwhelmed by the now realities of my life. How can someone infiltrate the values of our marriage? What ever happen to commitment? What happened to the covenant? What happened to when you told me you would never hurt me? What happened to my marriage? How did I become a mother of two, unemployed, living in lodging with a man that would rather be with another woman miles and miles away?

How in the world? I am functioning like a gun with bullets in it. Every day my husband spins me and I worry that this maybe the day I lose it. The day that I finally fire back at his betrayal. The day that I finally have enough strength to get up from here and leave this invisible jail you have created. Can love hold you to a lie? Can love make you look beyond the outright betrayal? Can love erase the pornographic photos of his lover spread eagle? Can love hold my head up when people I just met know the realities of this lie my husband has built? Can I ever see that love don't love here anymore? Here I am celibate for over 2 years while my husband…the man I bore 2 children for was living a sex karma sutra life from the comfy confines of his Osan home. Gallivanting around as if he didn't have a very valid marriage license or that he wasn't just in our Hickam AFB kitchen crying. Crying and trying to reassure me that he would never cheat again. Tell me this day-to-day unfolding of the lies of my husband is just an Ashton Kutcher Punk episode…with his woman on the side as a hired actress. Tell me that I don't have to one day tell my daughters that their father didn't just commit adultery once but 3 times in 6 years.

His excuse is I am a war vet and you don't know the things I have seen and gone through. I didn't know serving our country gave you the right to commit adultery. I didn't know that serving our country gave you the right to treat me the way you do. Yet, I come back to the same question why do you allow him to repeat his behavior? If his own Mama is saying you should pack up and leave…why are our bags not packed? Why are you still here daily going through emotional abuse while he eats the food you cook, while you clean the clothes he wears, and while he won't even wash a cup he uses? Marchet, you know better…you know that he doesn't love you. You have always said "the moment someone shows you who they really are believe them!" Why don't you believe him? He doesn't love you? In fact, he hates you? His daily actions prove that to be so. You are the only example your daughters have. Be true to yourself and do the right thing. You are not his priority and you haven't been his priority for a while. As Spike Lee wrote in School Daze …" WAKE UP!!!!!...WAKE UP!!!!!.... WAKE UP!!!!!! "YOU ARE WORTH MORE THAN THIS!!!

In all your ways acknowledge him, and he will make your paths straight. – **Proverbs 3:6**

A Day After Independence Day

As I reflect on "Independence Day" I can't help but ask myself if I'm Independent in my life.

1. Free from outside control; not depending on another's authority
2. Not depending on something else for strength or effectiveness; freestanding

"If you have been doing you, I'm going to do me!"-
FREE by Destiny Child

A day after Independence Day…July 5th he comes home and gives me the paperwork to sign. NO hello…NO how

The Confessions Of Church Girls

was your day…he just goes straight in and points out where I need to sign and where I'm supposed to put our passport numbers etc. Ladi dadi da…I'm not in shock but I would be a liar if I said that my heart didn't hurt. I just got done wishing 3 people a Happy Anniversary on Facebook. Now right after my Facebook Happy Anniversary posts my very own husband walks through the door and shoves the written reality that my own marriage is going down the toilet. I couldn't help but feel hurt, frustrated, and some what a failure. Here I thought I did everything to keep my marriage going but it didn't keep random women out of the bed with my husband. It didn't stop my husband from calling me a fat cow or telling me that the sound of my voice makes him sick. That's what years and multiple times of forgiveness gets me. Some will interject but you married the fool in the beginning not even telling Pastor about your decision. Yup…that was me. I was the one who ran into the arms of a man that promised to love me forever. The same man that I shared all my insecurities with and all my childhood pain. The one I told I only wanted to be married once. The one who told me he only wanted to be married once too.

Now here I am with nothing to show for it. Just vivid pictures of infidelity and a heart I am trying to protect from the overflow of hatred that is pounding on the walls of my heart. This can't be real but it was. He finally put the dagger completely through my heart. I have accepted it now and all the fight in me has gone. It's hard to fight for someone that has caused you so much pain. So, for my daughters I was STRONG and I gathered my tears. For they are the two BEST things I got out of this entire rollercoaster ride. A roller coaster ride of marriage that was full of lies and betrayals. I tried to throw my hands up and roll with the punches but you can only get bruised up for so long. I have to let go and move on…some may argue (including myself) that I should have done this a long time ago. Well, I didn't and today is the day it finally goes down.

So, I paused and went back on Facebook and Pastor Jamal Bryant happen to post this as his status:

Moving on is expensive but…….staying put is way 2

costly!

I couldn't help to wonder if in that very moment Pastor Jamal Bryant had a camera pointing directly into my life…lol. I knew however that the reality of the matter is that he didn't at that very moment I needed that. I have been banging my head out trying to figure out how financially I would be able to do all of this. I had no savings and no plan B. At the time it even seemed as if I had nothing in the natural as well but I made up my mind that I would do what I needed to do any way.

I remember so clearly that this was a very difficult time for me. It's one thing when the person you have committed your life to wants to leave but it's another thing when verbal abuse is attached to the situation. I lost myself in the process of him trying to lose me. My mind couldn't wrap my head around the fact that the vows we said that included "to death do us part" were just words he spoke. I also dealt with the reality of being a church girl. I now carried the extra burden of having to deal with the fact that not only was I going through a divorce but I didn't plan for this. I thought by me marrying someone that didn't want anything to do with church and accepting him for him would somehow guarantee my marriage to work. Right??? Wrong!!! That was absolutely wrong.

I loved my husband unconditionally but I wasn't enough for him. He felt the need to allow himself to violate our marriage and live his life as if he wasn't married. Leaving me…this "church girl" to digest the fact that it's was absolutely never worth me compromising my beliefs. Entangling yourself with someone that can say vows and commit to love and to be loyal to you on your wedding day. Yet, two children later and over a decade of marriage reveals a side of him that you never prepared for. This couldn't be the man that I married. This couldn't be the man who never argued with me the entire time we were dating. This couldn't be the man who carefully placed my engagement ring in a fortune cookie and the fortune read "Will you marry me?" This couldn't be the man who told me all the reasons he loved me prior to getting married but now had nothing good to say about me. This couldn't be the life that I chose to be a part of. What happened to the promises? Why are our daughters now having to deal with divorce and a single parent home? Lord, help me!

I'm not sure how many women, who are reading this book, have ever experienced anything like this and also did not have a Plan B. Maybe I'm the only woman that has experienced a betrayal that you didn't see coming. That was so fully committed and invested in your marriage and raising two young girls that you missed all the warning signs and found yourself on a journey that left you empty. I personally found myself overcome with anger and my mind became a vivid slide show of every word and promise that was spoken by my husband prior to him giving me these divorce papers the day after Independence Day. Did he plan it that way? Did he feel as if the day after would not hurt as bad? I can tell you personally that I definitely didn't feel FREE and the more I digest it all the more bound I became. I, Marchet Denise Fullum, couldn't believe this was my life. I slowly feel the walls closing in on me. Now I'm bound as I look at the life, I left for the life I willing accepted…I can't avoid the fact that now I must face the roots and realities that lead me to this point. I must dig in and my Pastor, my Mama, my daddies, family, or friends could not go through this process for me. I had a very hard road ahead of me that I could no longer avoid! This church girl had to go deeper than the surface of church and reach in for a true relationship. This church girl had to decide that choosing her own paths in life had proven time and time again to be an epic failure! This church girl had to realize that the only true FREEDOM would come through completely surrendering my will to God!

Some may argue that how can you declare you are FREE if you surrender and give your will to God! My answer simple and sweet would be is that's indeed what makes you FREE and I now know that not because I heard it across the pulpit, on a podcast, or listening to a live broadcasted sermon…this Church girl has learned that through giving it all to God. Every hurt, every disappointment, every misstep, every lie, every plan, every childhood experience, every adult experience, every single thing that was a hindrance and not good for me I surrendered it all. It was a unique and interesting time in my life because I had so many emotions going on at the same time but I PRESSED through how I felt and I willing share my experiences in this book and through my Blog "The Confessions of Church Girls." For what I know for sure is you can't hold in the lessons you learn for your lessons are not intended just for you. There is so much power when we let our life lessons speak to others so they can avoid, conquer, and overcome what was intended to keep them bound. God desires each of us to live a life of FREEDOM! My prayer

that through my transparency you will see you can make it too and you will PRESS THROUGH to live your BEST LIFE!

Come to me, all you who are weary and burdened, and I will give you rest. – **Matthew 11:28**

I Ask Myself

I ask myself where did I go wrong...why is my marriage dwindling away with my waistline.? How come I was there for everyone else and now I feel alone in a sense. Don't get me wrong it's not that I don't have the "FAITHFUL" few...it's that I feel so naked, so stupid, so ashamed! I was the one who believed in being faithful, in forgiving, in working things out. Now I feel like the one with egg all over her face as people are laughing. Some moments in the day I feel like "my latter will be greater" ...then other moments I just cry. Cry because my heart hurts in places where I can't even touch. Hurt because I can't quite understand WHY all of this is happening to me. I wonder if maybe I wasn't a good enough wife? Maybe I wasn't doing what I needed to do? Maybe I tried to change him too much? Or maybe I just changed in the process?

I think it would be easier to digest if I could pinpoint what I actually did wrong and could pinpoint where it actually broke. However, I can't explain another woman knowingly sleeping with a married man for a year. I can't imagine my husband being with different women and then saying to me "I just don't like you!" Really??? The sad part is I keep wishing that some way or somehow MY MARRIAGE WOULD HAVE WORK! What about all the prophecies? Maybe I was dumb enough to believe? Maybe I should have left a long time ago? Maybe???

I sit on my laptop to release because I honestly think I may eventually just run out of tears. Not because I shouldn't cry or don't want to cry anymore but because I possibly could have cried so much that that my body is incapable of producing any more tears. What happened to me? I'm now in my 40s, I'm practically a virgin again, and every now and then I'm lonely. What happened to my best friend? What happened to the love we had?

Now I daily fight to not allow, "hate" to consume my heart. It's hard for me not to hate someone who has taken 11 years of my life and can end it with "I don't even like you!" I've seen that junk in movies but I never thought in a million years I would be that chic. Guess what? In 2011 I heard those words and I became that chic. The chic so broken hearted that it was ridiculous. The chic that most would expect me to have something to say right back to him. Sometimes the hurt that penetrates your life causes you to become numb and you become just tired in general. Tired of believing that things would get better. Tired of being verbally abused. Tired of tolerating what was never acceptable. Just tired of it all.

I've lived my life based on prophetic words and right now I'm not sure what to think. What do you think when your life is dissolving? What do you think when you are standing on Styrofoam in the middle of an ocean just praying that I don't completely tip over? Praying that I can maintain this balancing act that I have done for so many years. I don't even feel like talking to any of my friends any more about it. I'm that emotionally battered person that doesn't have any upbeat quotes or clichés to say. I'm the worst downer you could ever be around right now because I am consumed with a pain I can't fully describe. I'm pretty sure it has been here for years but NOW it is forcing what I have mastered suppressing for years to come up to the surface. The scary part is I know only God could help me not bubble over before now.

If my hand, with all five fingers, could be an avatar in my chest and remove the existing pain that is overwhelming me like a non-curable cancer. If I had something I could drink or if the simple clicking of my slippers could fast-forward me beyond right now. I, Marchet Denise Fullum, would gladly press fast forward to excuse myself from this pain.

I can't help but think about all the people I thought I was encouraging during their difficult times. Only to realize that although I was completely sincere my efforts could have made the pain worst. I've had some of my closest friends, not intentionally, but without them even realizing it…say some things that made me feel worse. I don't blame them because I realize that they really just want the best for me. It frustrates them to see me in pain and also to see me so hurt. I guess that is how life is you begin to see things differently as you go through things you only had to coach someone else through. I am better because of it and my next encounter with someone in pain will cause me not to feel like I have to necessarily say anything. Sometimes the best antidote is silently just being there. I apologize to all the people that in my infancy of dealing with people in pain I said what I thought was right but didn't pause to acknowledge long enough the real pain they were going through. I also apologize for every time I used the scriptures to encourage or show right and didn't allow LOVE to be the pretreatment chaser. It was not intentional and I realize more than ever how going through a situation can give you great wisdom.

Let us not lose heart in doing good, for in due time we will reap if we do not grow weary. – **Galatians 6:9**

Check Your Price Tag

Last night I don't know when I actually fell to sleep. The last thing I remember I put my head under the cover and cried from the bottom of my soul. I had my encouragement playlist on iTunes playing in the background and I reached out to God. I asked God to forgive me, to help me, and to direct my paths. For I have found myself in a place where I have nothing else but God. I know nothing else can help me! Nothing else can take the pain away and correct whatever is within me that keeps bringing me to this place. If I hear one more time you are a great person, an incredible woman, mother, etc., etc., etc. I am going to go straight Looney Tunes.

How can a man tell you all those things and then still not want you? WHATEVER is what I say at the top of my lungs! My insides are having a thumping session of disappointment and my mind is a non-stop replay of all my life events that have led me to this. OMG! OMG! OMG! There has to be something wrong in me. Who would still be here? Who wouldn't get the point? Who wouldn't know that they were all those things before the perpetrator tried to declare it?

It seems as if after I found out my husband was cheating that our beautiful home in Italy transformed into a war zone. My husband was caught and now every opportunity he had he jumped at the opportunity to say something mean. As he purposely worked to push me out. It got to a point where all the scriptures I had learned while growing up in church and even the catch all phrase "Grace and Peace" were no longer my first choice for word exchanges with my husband.

Our basement downstairs became his hide away and preferred place to reside at the time. It was also the place where our daughter's toys and big play items resided. Yet with each passing day a bed was added and most of his personal items followed. He would retreat to the basement usually after he dropped a couple of hurtful bombs directly at me. Usually, these bombs were sent with his famous line "don't unpack all the boxes because they are just going to come and pack them all back up." Then my husband of almost 7 years went down to the basement and slammed the door because he had an attitude. Who does that and who says that? Not someone who loves you!

I would get so mad that I couldn't see straight. Yup this church girl lost it and went off because I couldn't believe this man would have us come all the way over to Italy only to have us to go all the way back to Hawaii. This chocolate church girl then proceeded to say some choice cuss words that I have deliberately decided to leave out of this book. I didn't even know I could put cuss words together that well. As I reflected back on it, I wasn't sure if anger alone helped line those cuss words up so eloquently or if the feeling of betrayal assisted. Either way at the time I just figured the Lord would have to forgive me. I then tried to justified it by saying there were no words in the human vocabulary that would suffice for how I felt outside of cuss words. Then once again I go on Facebook and saw the below:

"If you're NOT being treated with love & respect, check your "price tag". Perhaps you have marked yourself

down. It's you who tells people what you are worth BY WHAT YOU ACCEPT. Get off the "clearance rack" and get behind the glass where they keep all the "valuables." The bottom line is...."value" yourself more. Repost if you like...You might help someone get off the clearance rack."

Lord whoever wrote this...well said...well said!!! God knew I needed to see this before I went postal on his selfish inconsiderate behind. It made me take a much-needed pause. I began to tell myself that starting right then I was going to check my price tag and begin putting myself behind the glass where "valuables" are kept!

As I made the decision to know my own worth. The process of going back home to Hawaii had to begin. As silly as it may sound even the smallest things become an issue when two people are angry. So here we are now rumbling through the hundreds of DVDs we had. This one is yours this one is mine. As my house becomes a murder scene...the very life of my marriage is under direct scrutiny and investigation. As my daughters and I prepare to leave what I thought was going to be a "NEW BEGINNING" and start again just the 3 of us. I can't help but cry as my very life seems to be crumbling in front of me.

My oldest daughter just turned 6 years old and while she was consumed with her presents, I pulled out a DVD that I had never seen yet "The Secret Life of Bees". It spoke volumes to me not about just right now but about how in spite of what may happen in your life you have to KEEP ON LIVING! For me I just can't keep living for myself but I have to keep living for my two daughters. It's my responsibility to ensure that adult decisions don't interfere with their innocent childhood. So, I finally decided to make the very difficult adult decision to exit left.

Cast your cares on the LORD and he will sustain you; he will never let the righteous fall. – **Psalm 55:22**

THE PROCESS

Bust The Windows Out Your Car

WHY? WHY? WHY? WHY? WHY? DANGIT!!! I gave you almost 11 years of my life...2 kids...maintained your home...and never once cheated on you! Then you...YES...you Mr. Fullum could play house with this no morale having bimbo. Without ever once considering the price you would have to pay. I just don't get it! I just don't understand! I just don't think that I deserve this abuse!

Yet I stayed and I stayed. Then you abuse me and kick me with your action and words because you selfishly know that I love you! Although you swear you don't know what love is...you knew enough to keep me here. As you continued to act as if you were so confused. Then to not admit that if I didn't find your cell phone on the back of the toilet that you would have continued this double life! Lord ...I need you to help me to remain calm and to not cause him harm. Lord, I need you to direct my paths...Selah.

These were the words and conversation that occurred almost on a regular basis after I found out my husband had brought me all the way to Italy with both of our daughters. Though the two paragraphs above didn't always sound the same way the hurt I felt was consistently communicated. It was hard to comprehend why my husband would bring us from my family in Hawaii, even though he knew he had been cheating with another woman for over a year while he was TDY in Korea. Wouldn't it have made sense to just tell me when he was in Korea. Why did he feel the need to lie and continue to lie? How could he expose me to possible STDs and a hurtful humiliation in Italy. It just didn't add up. So, I found myself listening to Jasmine Sullivan in an attempt to soothe my pain but instead I found myself ANGRY and wanting immediate revenge. Yup…this CHURCH GIRL had no scriptures left and I no longer felt like praying for a man that could possibly hurt me this bad.

Jasmine Sullivan's song, "I'll Bust the Windows Out Your Car", was playing on repeat, tears flowing down my cheeks, and the sound of anything else was intentionally mute in my mind! I sat there on the basement steps numb and stiff like a statue. I wasn't quite sure what would happen next, I just knew when he finally woke up, I wanted him to feel pain too!

I remember trying to mentally sift through the lies and decipher where any TRUTH remained. I became nauseated as I could no longer stomach his venomous choices. Vivid images of his mistress spread eagle on my computer screen and for some reason nothing from Genesis to Revelation brought my hurting heart comfort in that moment. I remember also feeling less than his Grey Denali. His four wheeled, gas guzzling, pride, and joy. I knew without a doubt that if I busted the windows and left a shattering reality for him...he would be devastated. Yet, overwhelmed with so much hurt that still wasn't enough...

So, there I sat butcher knife tightly gripped and I had convinced myself I had enough! Yup, you read right "butcher knife" tightly gripped!!!! I CONFESS...Marchet Denise Fullum had been pushed to the edge! I had dedicated my life to this man, prayed for us, fasted for us, changed my last name, gave birth to two beautiful girls, miscarried one child, and yet I somehow couldn't avoid a marriage filled with so much deceit!

I was the one holding the home front down while you were TDY for a year not just serving our country but "serving" another chic. All along calling home, sending letters, and packages as if our love and our family was most important in your life! I grip tighter!!! Hand sweating, heart beating, and my mind became an HD slideshow of picture-perfect moments we shared! Only to be abruptly interrupted by these new F.B.I. (Females beside "I") secret files I was now receiving in bulk! I grip tighter!

Tears still flowing as I've lost track of how long I've been sitting on the basement steps! Overwhelmed by the invisible yet painfully obvious lines of separation that have become permanent residents in what I once knew as OUR home. I GRIP TIGHTER! My heart beats faster! I'm overwhelmed with loneliness and I'm 7729.04 miles from home...Hawaii! I was angry.... very, very, very angry!

I had sat through numerous marriage counseling sessions, heard countless times a series of selfishly driven lies, and now I was tired of being the CHURCH GIRL! Tired of "turning the other cheek" as he kept pouring heavy servings of manipulation upon what should have been pure! I nakedly reveal this portion to you because while being the best of friends prior to marriage, intimately exchanging our wedding vows, embracing our 1st and second child...I never thought my story would have a chapter of CONFESSION like this!

Yet as I type and pour out my reality, I realize one of my many TESTimonies is that I didn't bust the windows out his truck nor did I try to physically duplicate the pain I felt! Instead, when he finally opened the basement door half asleep and immediately caught off guard...as he saw me red eyed, focused, and intensely gripping the stainless-steel butcher knife... I began to laugh, I got up, and walked away from what WAS NOT IN ME TO DO!

It seemed as if it was the longest walk ever up those

basement stairs but I knew without a shadow of a doubt that "someone had PRAYED for me had me on their mind took a little time to PRAY for me!" By the time I made it to my room I BROKE...and a river of tears rolled from my cheeks to my lonely sheets. I knew the only thing that had been cut was my heart!

I vividly write the realities of this day for those of you who have WOUNDS, HURT, and PAIN. The type of WOUNDS, HURT, and PAIN that resides deep in your hearts and runs throughout the corridors of your minds. The type of WOUNDS, HURT, and PAIN that human hands can't quite reach! I take the time to type this out to without a doubt make it clear to many that YOU may never know what an individual is dealing with on a second-by-second basis! It was INDEED the LOVE of God, the FAITHFUL few, the sincere prayer, phone calls, and "just because" interjections during this time that kept me from drowning in depression!

It was those timely reminders that the IRON in my life would speak with unconditional LOVE:

"I think you are absolutely amazing and equally as beautiful. I wanted to tell you that in spite of everything you have gone through and are going through, God is still God. And even in our confusion and questions wondering why did it have to happen this way, He's there waiting patiently while his perfect plan unfolds. You may not understand it all now, but one day in His perfect timing it will all be revealed. And knowing the kind of God that we serve, it will be "for our good." All I can say is to keep going and keep moving. I'll be right here with you."

NOW I grip tighter to God, the FAITHFUL few, and the IRON in my life! For I know my TEST is now my TESTimony! I am still STANDING, LEARNING, GROWING, & definitely HEALING! I'm no longer numb, holding my breath, or sitting on basement stairs! I grip my keyboard tighter and allow my CONFESSIONS to openly flow so that someone else may know they are not alone! YOU CAN make it through your hardest times and what appears to be your hardest test!

If you fall to pieces in crisis…There wasn't much to you in the first place. —**Proverbs 24:10 MSG**

Blessed is the man who perseveres under trial, because when he has stood the test, he will receive the crown of life that God has promised to those who love him. – **James 1:12**

Putting Things in The Right Perspective

Over this past week I have been reflecting and thinking about how I look at things. I have found that when I'm faced with an issue or circumstance in my life that it is imperative for me to take control of my thoughts. Let yourself for a minute think about a time when you thought "I just can't make it through this" or "Man these hurts so much when will it end?" The most frequent one-word question during these times is "Why?"

The funny thing about "Why" is we ask it and sometimes we don't get an immediate response. What I have learned is that the way you get through something is by placing one foot in front of the other and moving forward. It takes you getting up from where you are…whether it's across your bed with tears running down your face or substituting your pain for food. Let me pause really quick right there. I know for many we support curves and full-sized women and I'm in no way killing Plus Size PRIDE. However, "for ME" I found that I was filling my void with an occasional (or frequent LOL) Molten Chocolate Cake with Carmel on top from Chili's or a warm cheeseburger after 8pm. Sometimes a blackened Opah fish sandwich with homemade fries from this cute little restaurant conveniently placed right across the street from my home.

I CONFESS (which some of you aren't ready to hear) that I so desired not to become a "ho", while still being married and while still coming home every night to an empty bed. That might be too real for some of you but trust me I'm getting to a real point. I had seriously thought that because I was so angry about all that had taken place in my marriage that it would be easy for me to put on my "GET IT GIRL" dress and sooth my pain in the arms of another temporary setback. Yup…that's what it really is for us CHURCH GIRLS that know better but have allowed our lives to spin out of control. It becomes easy to justify the "sin" that we now conveniently make excuses for.

I would be lying if I didn't tell you that I went through serious withdrawals. Many nights I cried myself to sleep as I fought pass the sinful desires to just go get a temporary relief and instead to seek God's face for what He really wanted for my life. Did I mention it was a rough period because there was "few" that I could actually turn to during this time period in my life? Most people wanted to quote me a scripture (and don't get me wrong I know the word is quick and powerful and sharper than any two-edged swords… but ummmm that wasn't where I was at that time). I was still a young woman who had very fine options calling me on the phone but I had to make the decision that I wanted off this roller coaster ride of disappointments, lies, and betrayal. I need to be buckled into the realities of what God truly intended for me. Although many may disagree a dildo or a man that was not my husband was not the answer.

For me the answer was CONFESSING to God that I, Marchet Denise Fullum, couldn't walk through this life alone. I needed my perspective upgraded and I needed the God I heard so much about while growing up to prove himself to me not just inside the church walls but outside the church walls as well. I was doing something that was not popular in 2012/2013 I chose to completely SURRENDER my will and my pain to God. I do CONFESS that I never wanted to write about this part of my journey and for months now I have struggled with allowing my 10 fingers to engage with my Apple keyboard…BUT it is way overdue.

It's time for me to put my experiences out there so people don't think that a life of PEACE is not obtainable. So that people can drown the lies and myths that roar in the midst of so many "church" conversations that Christians can't have fun. I have fun because I STRIPPED myself from the expectation of people and fell into the arms of God. I had to be careful to avoid those who were comfortable with a life filled with compromise and excuses. I knew that it was essential for me to stay focused because my mind was warring with me and making me want to accept the fact that I would not be able to live a life of celibacy.

If I sat at my computer right now and typed that it was

all a breeze and that my decision to do things Gods way vs. how I felt was easy that would be a flat out, lie. What I can say is the closer I got to God and the more I eliminated people and things that were going against my goal the easier it got. I learned that even though my secret placed screamed to be fulfilled that I could press through it. I knew how it felt to compromise myself and fulfill the screams and yearnings of my secret place. I knew that doing things my way or getting a quick climax was not going to carry me through the many days ahead. I had to decide to take that energy and apply it to preparing myself for what lied ahead. I had to deal with some things, to accept some truths about myself, and to make up in my mind that no matter what "get out of what seemed to be a jai free card" the world tried to present me that I would remain focus on my goal for life.

I already knew what compromise felt and looked like. I knew what it looks like to go against the truth of God's word and to act as if I never knew Gods truth. I knew how easy it was to position myself in a way where we would end up naked and how easy it seemed to just ask for forgiveness only to repeat the sin again. At the end of the day, when I was ready to be honest with myself I realized and accepted sin was never worth it. Let me interject this book is a transparent overview of my life as a Church Girl. I now know how easy it is to compromise God's word and I have made it one of my life missions to help other church girls and woman in general through the transparency of my story. What I've learned is not debatable for I know how it feels to go down a road that seems right but ends in pain, embarrassment, and disappointment.

I'm indeed a work in progress and I am daily learning the power of putting things in perspective. My sincere prayer is that the honesty and uniqueness of who I am will touch those often over looked right where they are. I have always been an out the box type of CHURCH GIRL and for many years I wasn't proud of who I was! What I am learning is that by putting things in the right perspective I am not only giving myself permission to sort through my life but I am giving others the permission to CONFESS they are a work in progress too.

Wouldn't it be wonderful if we all could put things in perspective? If we could willingly extend our hands to each other with a sincere desire to see each other reach their full potential. How many hearts would be mended? How many wounded CHURCH GIRLS would regain the volume in their vocal cords and declare they are putting things into perspective. We each have a story and my story will continue to be shared through THE CONFESSION OF CHURCH GIRLS...for every time my 10 fingers hit these Apple keys, I'm putting one foot in front of the other and finally not apologizing for the content or my CONFESSIONS! In the words of Tamar Braxton... "Aint nobody got time for that!" I'm putting things in the right PERSPECTIVE...now tag your it!

> Peace, I leave with you; my peace I give you. I do not give to you as the world gives. Do not let your hearts be troubled and do not be afraid. – **John 14.27**

Marchet Denise Fullum

A Small Broom & Dust Pan

One thing I am extremely grateful for is that not all of "the FAITHFUL few" were raised in church. Before some of you get offended...just breathe and take a moment to digest the story I'm about to tell. I have a wonderful friend name Janiel. Janiel is Buffalo born and raised! Our paths crossed when I was working in Ft. Belvoir, VA for AAFES. The initial common factor we both had is our sincere over the top love for the one and only BORIS KODJOE! Back then he wasn't the loving husband and father we know him to be now...but he was this FINE, TALL, SEXY, SINGLE, YOUNG man who happened to be modeling for Polo.

Wouldn't you know I just happened to be the Sales Area Manager for the Men's department at the Ft. Belvoir PX. I was beyond thrilled to get all the life-sized signing and advertisement that had Boris's chiseled body decorated all over them...ooooooh yes...lol...OK, OK, OK! I'm back! Janiel and I started up a conversation one day as she came to my office and realized I had a shrine of all the previous Polo signage that Boris was on. No exaggeration my office could have been the National Boris Museum. It was from that point on Janiel and I hit it off. We were opposite in many ways but an incredible friendship began right there in the Men's Department.

So fast forward Janiel and I discovered we both had a second love and that love was dancing. Now most of my dancing up to this point was only in church. I grew up during a time where secular music was "of the devil." There absolutely would not have been any "wobbling" allowed back then, no 93.9 FM, and definitely no DJs. I grew up during a time where the organ player was the DJ and the Holy Spirit was the choreographer of any dancing taking place. So initially even me entertaining the idea of going to a club was A LOT! However, club DREAM in DC was not your average club. It was built with extreme class and thought. The moment you walked in you weren't entering your normal club scene. This was evident by the often mile long line just to get in. It was 4 stories high not counting the open roof top area where you may bump into a local NFL player, an Executive, a hustler, or many other types of men. Each floor had a theme whether it was R&B, Hip Hop, Reggae, House, etc. At club Dream you were guaranteed to find a floor that suited your needs for the moment, hour, or the night.

This particular night the one and only Boris Kodjoe was hosting the event. It seemed as if every obstacle that could prevent us from entering into the club presented itself. However, you already know Janiel and I was going to do whatever it took to meet Boris Kodjoe. Our determination paid off because after enduring the line and getting in we soon found out that Boris Kodjoe was on the 4th floor. Not only was he on the 4th floor he was also the bartender. As we both got closer to the bar this church girl was doing flips inside. The closer we got the more reality clicked in that ummmmmm I would have to order a drink from Boris Kodjoe.

Any other person probably would have been cool, calm, and ready...but nope not this church girl. By the time I got up there and the one and only Boris Kodjoe asked me what I wanted to drink. I looked him in his eyes and said..."I LOVE YOU!" While I was still numb, he did a cute chuckle and I honestly can't even tell you what I ordered. All I know is instantaneously I felt like OMG I need proof that I met BORIS KODJOE...duh??? LOL...so I asked him to sign my purse and he did! Corny as that was, I walked away from the bar no longer hearing the music but clutching my purse that I now believed eternally held a piece of BORIS KODJOE...LMBO!!! In my mind nothing could ever go wrong again...I just told Boris Kodjoe I loved him, I was in his presence, he made me a drink, signed my purse, and was ultimately leaving with me via my purse. Boy, the scenarios we create in our heads, LOL, but at that moment everything I just wrote was my reality.

You would think that after a night like that you and your friend would leave the club. You would think you would go back to your friend's car and it would safely be right where you left it. Right? Of course! Who would ever think after a night of being at Dream night club and meeting BORIS KODJOE that you would ever return back to Janiel's car only for the window to be broken. Let me clarify when I say broken, I'm talking about someone intentionally took a hard object and broke Janiel's window. Leaving tons of little shattered glass on the seats, the floor, and outside Janiel's car.

It didn't just stop there...oh no of course not...they had stolen a bunch of valuable items that were in Janiel's car. I know...I know...I know...you didn't expect the story to go like this. Please trust me I didn't either. I had never...NEVER EVER...had that happen in my life nor had I experienced it. So of course, I'm feeling bad for Janiel because we drove her car and now the window is shattered and items were stolen. So, what do I do I pull out my little cell phone and go to call 911 and the next series of things Janiel proceeded to do has stuck with me until this very day.

She told me Chet hangs up the phone the police aren't going to do nothing to get my window fixed. Janiel then proceeded to pop the trunk and pulled out a SMALL BROOM AND DUST PAN! She then began to tell me in so many words that "things like this happens all the time where I'm from...Chet you can't let it BREAK YOU...YOU JUST GOTTA PICK UP THE PIECES AND KEEP IT MOVING! I stood there literally floored because I knew if the tables had been turned and we had been driving my car. There wouldn't have been a SMALL BROOM AND DUST PAN in the trunk!

I shared this story to say this. Sometimes we are so quick to judge people because they weren't raised the same way we were. In fact, some of us have missed out on valuable friendships because we think everyone has to be like us. On that night I learned a valuable lesson. One thing was that <u>everything that happens doesn't have to break you or break your spirit</u>. You have to keep things in perspective. Especially when there is no immediate fix other than popping the trunk, pulling out a SMALL BROOM AND DUST PAN, and sweeping up the shattered pieces.

Janiel knew the window could be replaced and she was also prepared to MOVE ON! How different would our lives be if we just popped the trunk and pulled out the SMALL BROOM AND DUST PAN...so we could MOVE ON? How much time do we allow ourselves to let one moment change a great night or a great day? Janiel was determined to cherish the night we had. I remember so clearly; she bent down and began sweeping up the shattered pieces. She popped the trunk again and put the SMALL BROOM AND DUST PAN back. Then she turned on the radio and said Chet get in. The whole way home Janiel was singing, laughing, and jamming! She left what someone else intended for her evil right where the car was originally parked. Janiel MOVED ON!

Today I just wanted to encourage someone and say we aren't always able to change current circumstances. A lot of your realities are real and sometimes may seem hard to endure. I just want you to allow yourself to keep a SMALL BROOM AND DUST PAN close by so you can immediately begin to sweep up the shattered things that were intended to break you down. Janiel showed me the importance of being EQUIPPED and the beauty in MOVING ON! Janiel, I want to personally thank you for this lesson and many others I can't wait to share! You never quoted a scripture but your life was a living example of what I was taught in church yet I had struggled to apply! I love you BIG for accepting this Church Girl and teaching me some real-life lessons outside the church walls. Everything around you don't have to be exactly like you. You can establish an "IRON SHARPENS IRON" relationship even with those who aren't Church Girls. A lot of times we think because we were raised in church that we are the only ones that can teach valuable lessons or pour into the lives of others. It's essential that we open up our minds and lives to the possibilities of those we may think we are better than. You never know the lessons you may learn that will change your life forever. In all the years I was in church I didn't grasp the truth behind a SMALL BROOM AND DUST PAN. Thank God my FAITHFUL few is not limited to church attendance but orchestrated through true life experiences. IRON REALLY SHARPENS IRON whether the iron was raised in the church or raised in Buffalo.

Iron sharpeneth iron; so, a man sharpeneth the countenance of his friend. -**Proverbs 27:17**

Maui

Honestly, I know I wouldn't have made it without God. As I sit here and type. Acknowledging that I am over weight, depressed, and still digesting the fact that I never imagined I would be lonely, celibate, and still married at this point in my life. I look at myself and can't believe that the extra fat holding my laptop up right now isn't going away when I hit the delete button on my keyboard. Nope it's me without any filters, cropping, or fancy camera trick that can somehow just show people what I want them to see. My hormones are raging an instead of going out and having sex with any man that looks and smells good. I have replaced an orgasm for an occasional burger, onion rings, or anything that fills this void I know exist.

I haven't addressed it I just stay busy. Constantly trying to live up to everyone standards although it seems they maybe standards I have carried along in my life since childhood. Something similar to the Charlie Brown character that carried around his blanket. Now that I am in my 40s, I am still dragging along things I just don't want to deal with. I mean honestly how do you deal with a 7-year divorce process? How do you deal with the fact that your current living situation with both of your daughters is less than before you got married? How do you look around and notice that most of the people you call friends are also over weight, or single, or married but don't have enjoyable sex lives? How does this work or happen amongst those of us who declare Jesus as our Lord and Savior? Since being in Maui I have asked myself a lot of hard questions. I wonder why you would stay in a marriage so long with someone who flat out disrespects you? Why do you keep yourself open to people who could care less about you? Why do you keep attaching yourself to these men whose mothers stay connected but never want to take accountability for the deceptive sons they have?

I mean at the end of the day whose fault, is it? The church girl or the mother for falling in love and having children with a man that was still a boy. How hard will I have to continue to work to pay for an "I do" that felt like voodoo that forever cursed my chocolate life? How long do I have to be the responsible one who ensures my daughters are both taken care of and often survives off of 4 hours of sleep? How often will my heart be a revolving door that even those from my past occasionally travel through? I ask myself do I want my daughters repeating my example? As well as, what example did I have? See it gets real sticky when you really want to get to the root of the matter. There's no way around someone feelings not getting hurt for we are never really sure where the dirt will land.

I regress and realize that I can't fall back into the same position I was already in. Obviously, this trip is bigger than Me and I must take the time to sort through the issues of my life. The uniquely painful thing to me is that as much as I enjoy getting naked it's a completely different thing when it is parallel to this book I write.

A part of me is so angry at myself for being the type of girl that believed in fairy tales. For being the type of woman that sees the best in a man and believes that if you love a man, he will love you back. I had to get to a point where I allowed myself to really digest where I am right now. For 5 days I have been on one of the most beautiful islands. Just me....no kids...no friends...no man (but if I was perfectly honest, I sure wish one was here) ...nobody! Just me solo. In a paid for condo timeshare. You would think as a single mother I would be super excited at the possibility of just being alone. However, the reality was I have been alone long enough.

I may be the only person in America who has ever felt this way but I can and have had people around me for the past seven years...but deep down inside I have been so very lonely. I am the queen of making it seem like everything is ok. With planning a great event and making sure my life is jammed packed with busy things too. So, I decided to jot down a list of Me, Myself, & I things to do and consider.

1. I need to find out what I need and want out of life.
2. I need to know my worth and not settle for anything less.
3. I need to remember that God has a plan for my life.

4. I need to know that I am a direct, living, and walking example to my two daughters.
5. I need to know that where one man refuses to sleep another man will rest in peace.
6. I need to get myself healthy.
7. I need to filter out the wrong people out of my life-everyone that doesn't help to move me forward.
8. I need to figure out what my passions still are.
9. I need to do for myself as much as I did for ex-husband and every other man that has been attached to my life.
10. I need to remember that my life isn't over.
11. I need to guard my mind and only put in it what will help me and not what will cause a backup.
12. I need to know that there is a big world out there with people who are willing to treat me the way I am supposed to be treated.
13. I need to know that God is my source.
14. I need to discipline myself.

Oftentimes as women we just need to fully digest that we are blessed. Sometimes it takes us doing what we're supposed to be doing and aligning ourselves up with God's word to realize that we are strong, we can conquer, and we have work to do. The list above was made in Maui. I debated about including it because I know there will be someone with a critical eye that will point out something that should be on there or something they don't feel should have been included. For that very reason I left my real-life transparent list to encourage so many of you women out there to just start somewhere. Your list might not be the same as someone else. Your list might not include anything related to God and church but trust me when I say there is something about just getting in motion. There is something about taking the fear of what other people think and just honestly evaluating yourself.

Nothing will ever be accomplished for the Kingdom of God or for your life if we don't bring to birth what God has instilled in us. This birthing process that we experience as single women or women in general spiritually is a direct parallel to the natural birthing process we should experience. It's time that we as women begin to share our wounds and battle scars. There is work in God's kingdom for us. We spend so much time on unnecessary things that we fail to realize that the clock is ticking. We need to learn from our past and press forward!

Often times that might mean that you can no longer put yourself on hold in an attempt to try and resuscitate a ministry that has not done the same for you.

Just like I had to digest the realities of my marriage I am also having to digest the realities of ministry, church, and being connected. To put it in a visual sense I feel like I need to expand and sort through some issues in life. If I have everything crammed into a studio apartment, then I limit myself to that. If I open myself up to the possibilities of more than I give myself room to sort and grow.

I'm not sure if this will make sense beyond myself but although the circumstances that got me away has brought pain and much disappointment, I don't think I would have otherwise left. I think I never really got to find out who I was because I have lived under this definition of who I was supposed to be. I was always being told I was good enough but being left behind. So, I kind of down played myself for years and started feeding myself the same thoughts. I got comfortable in Hawaii...comfortable to the point where I was so consumed with the work of church that my own life was going hay wire.

You would think that after all those years I would know who I was and would have had a definite vision. Sadly, I didn't. I lost myself in being and doing what was acceptable. Instead of being and doing what I felt was right for me. I am not at all saying that I know all things and that I am perfect needing no guidance. Nor am I watering down my experiences in Hawaii. I've just changed. I think anyone would change if they had to doggie paddle through some of the worst storms of their life. I often didn't even have a piece of wood to hold on to all I had was myself and my faith. I had to deal with some ugly truths about life, time, church, and myself.

I had to realize that the value of my life and my time was

an afterthought to many. I think that has been my biggest issue in life. I have not spoken up enough for things that were important to me. I blame myself for being passive when I know I need to be aggressive. I needed to not be afraid to proclaim that all wasn't well yet. As well as, without fear be able to declare that I was sorting through my life...being a mother...and trying to see what I actually even knew about being a wife.

I was grabbing the pieces of my life and going to God asking him to forgive me for ever putting any forms of a "priest" before him. If we are not careful church will become our God and we will swiftly lose grip of a true relationship with God. I personally know for myself now that I can go to God directly and I do not have to depend on others to do it for me. There's nothing quite as beautiful as your own personal relationship with God. Don't allow others to be your crutch or your excuse. Instead dig and surrender your all to God. Let God show you through his word and your time with him the realities of who he really is. You don't just have to be a church girl that attends church. You can be a church girl that loves God.

> Be strong and courageous. Do not fear or be in dread of them, for it is the LORD your God who goes with you. He will not leave you or forsake you. – **Deuteronomy 31:6**

It Took Me A Long Time to Get These Feet Off My Neck

It took me a long time to get these feet off my neck. The pressure of expectations and the intent to keep me stringed to the traditions that kept them bound for so long. I no longer can be the puppet of tradition as I remember the days where holiness was not a blurred reflection of a double life but a clear-cut consistent path. Ironically, I must CONFESS that I use to feel like I had to hold my tongue and not confront the inconsistency that I'm seeing more and more inside the church walls. In the streets they commonly refer to this as "game knows game" but in the church we see game and too often turn a blinds eye. Hmmmm and I often wonder why? Is it because our feet have the evidence of inappropriate living as the tracks of sin muddy the holy ground we are supposed to be standing on. Oh no I'm not referring to freshly redeemed saints but those "aints" perpetrating like "saints" who hide behind titles, positions, and how many years they've been in church. You know those been around for "years and years aints". The ones you would expect to be an example yet the funky scent from their undercover double lives is no longer ignorable.

Are you really supposed to be giving me an offering envelope as I catch your eyes engaging the booty of the sister that just walked down the aisle? Does being married still mean you sleep with just your wife or can you still work in ministry while making another woman climax? Do our "names" excuse us from having to repent? Is fornication (i.e., sex before marriage) still a NO NO…or is a little hit here, a little hit there, and a little hit everywhere ok because you "sure can teach that word" or "play that instrument"? So, you're a ministry coordinator at church but at night you pimp your wife's secret sexual addiction….am I understanding this all correctly? Hmmmmmm if I recall when I was a young girl in church "just a little leaven leavens the whole lump!"

If we're not careful the very word that was intended to SET US FREE will be used as a lynching device by those who have too quickly forgotten the lives they once lived! So instead of running for Jesus I confess I use to run and dance to the rhythmic expectations of others. Before long my legs, my arms, and my feet had been cloned to duplicate the life dance that led so many of them in circles for years. I watched their lives twirl out of control as they lied and said they were happy about the life that was void of true harmony. The fast-clanking sound of someone hitting a tambourine has been ushered away by an 8x10 piece of paper that lets us know what's supposed to happen next.

How many lives have to be tarnished from the truth being altered to protect the lives of those who use to be loud sounding trumpets? How much longer will we act as if we don't know homes are raggedy right within our very own leadership? The same leadership that once lead us but now find themselves suffocating in their own sin! I'm sure this chapter won't be popular as more people will try to make it literal instead of stopping and declaring "WE" have work to do!!!

I confess this church girl wants to enter into his gates with thanksgiving and enter into his courts with praise but I will no longer do it acting as if everything is ok. If we really love one another we would operate in truth instead of turning a blinded eye! How many lives have to be affected as accountability is no longer the standard? It's time for us within the churches to OPEN OUR EYES & get OUR lives together...GAME KNOWS GAME!

The above scenarios and mentions have become too familiar within our churches. We are losing ourselves and we are no longer being effective witnesses to those who actually come for their lives to be changed. The older I become and I'm allowed to obtain a closer look at the sad realities that occur within our churches I realize that the main problem is we no longer are keeping each other accountable. As our lives become contradictory standards that should not be duplicated.

I had to learn that everybody in the church isn't saved and I had to begin to put it all in perspective. I couldn't allow the behavior of others to begin to give me excuses to leave church or to alter my personal relationship with God. I write about this because I know the realities of this has affected so many people. I have seen so many people leave and we have to begin to stop this cycle. Love is the key. For it takes real love to hold others accountable. We can no longer turn a blind eye to matters that need to be addressed. GAME DOES KNOW GAME and this is one game that needs to end within the church walls. GAME OVER!

> You were running the race nobly. Who has interfered in (hindered and stopped you from) you're heeding *and* following the Truth? This [evil] persuasion is not from Him Who called you [Who invited you to freedom in Christ]. A little leaven (a slight inclination to error, or a few false teachers) leavens the whole lump [it perverts the whole conception of faith or misleads the whole church]. -**Galatians 5:7-9**

Broke Down...No Fight in Them...Hiding Behind the Curtains Believers

Those words came out of the mouth of my friend and brother Jemar Miller. I will never forget when I read the following:

"Just wanted you to know that I appreciate you! Why? If there's one thing, I can't stand is a broke down, no fight in them, hiding behind the curtain's believers. However, when I look at you and talk to you there are no visible signs of warfare! I appreciate that because I know the God that YOU serve is real. So that lets me know that the God I serve is real too because he is the Same, Yesterday, Today, Forever more for you and I. He's so good and faithful and by your example others will believe that He CAN and He WILL do what he says! We just have to trust and show-up willing! Take Care! Holla at a playa when you see me in the streets... Hottie

Hoo!"-JM"

I let Jemar know immediately that I would be quoting him in my book. I have no choice but to believe in the God and the Word I have deposited into my life. It has taught me that you can't live on snacks with God. You have to make sure you have a well-nourished spiritual life. It takes a combination of a lot of things. Sometimes it's just being quiet and allowing God to do a surgery so that God can minister to you directly. Other times for me it has been putting on my sneakers and workout clothes. I would then leave out the door and just walk. I didn't really know where I was going but I knew I needed some time to let it all go. Sometimes during the walk, I would be crying, sometimes I would be singing, sometimes I would be worshiping, sometimes reflecting where my life was, but it always ends with me feeling better spiritually and physically.

I am learning a lot about myself. I thought I had it pretty much together but I didn't. I forgot that regardless of my husband's action that I was supposed to be praying that he would know God and get his life right. The Bible says that he would be won over by me (his wife) and my actions. Well, when you try to fight and you are not allowing yourself to be spiritually nourished so you can get proper direction. Then it quickly goes from God's will to yours. I am learning and I know now that my ministry is not just boxed in teaching 7th through Young Adults but in teaching about relationships in general. Relationships in all areas and aspects of our life. From parent to child, child to friend, child to relatives, adults to relatives and friends, etc.

Our relationships affect our lives in so many ways. I see how my relationships prior to me getting married affected my marriage and my life. I had to daily rehearse and basically would wear out two of my favorite scriptures…Jeremiah 29:11 & Numbers 23:19. I love all the Bible but there is something about God has a plan just for YOU and God doesn't lie that always brings reassurance. I believe it to mean that God wouldn't say it if he wasn't going to do it. I realized I needed knowledge and I needed to be nourished in a lot of areas of my life. So, I had to learn to pray for my husband's salvation. Also, I pray that through all of this that God would make me into the woman that I'm supposed to be and that He would continue to guide my footsteps, to give me favor, to fight my battles, and to prepare a table for me in the presence of my enemies. My prayers for my husband will not stop even after our divorce because he will always be the father of our two daughters. I never thought that I would be open to continuing to pray for him after all the hurt, embarrassment, and pain I endured. However, I have grown and matured in areas that I thought I already had together. This Church Girl had to be broken so that I could now begin to live my best life and to let go of all the hate I had towards him. It's very hard to move forward if you don't allow yourself to sort through it all and deal with it. It was so essential that I properly did that because it wasn't just about us but we have two daughters that were being impacted by it all. If my motivation couldn't initially be because it was the right thing to do. Then I always had to keep my daughters as my motivation to do things the right way, to humble myself, and to allow God to do something within me. I had to learn to pray for myself just as much as I was "praying" for him. At this point in my life, I've determined that I Won't Stop and I Can't Stop!

The LORD will fight for you; you need only to be still." – **Exodus 14:14**

Spring Cleaning

For the past couple of days, I have been thinking about "SPRING CLEANING". I tried to avoid the subject but the more I tried to just shake the idea off it wouldn't leave my mind. So of course, I started doing some SPRING CLEANING in my townhouse...lol. I thought well surely this is heavy on my heart because this townhouse of mine is in some serious need of some SPRING CLEANING.

So, I started gutting out closets, making piles of things to give away, I ran across a couple of things that I had forgotten about, and I started putting things in new places throughout the house.

The more I cleaned the better I felt because some of the things I had started had been on my "to-do-list" waaaaaaaay too long. As I began to check things off of my list, I felt lighter in a sense because it was one less thing that I had to do. As I would finish one closet and then a room. I would step out of the room to get a good view...and a big Kool-Aid smile would decorate my face.

I felt better as PROGRESS was being made. I had begun to absorb the benefits of doing what had been put off for waaaaaaaaaaay too long. The more I did the more I wanted to do more because I could see the changes.

What became even more rewarding is when my two daughters and my brother Glenn began to rave almost in harmony on how much they like the changes. As well as, commenting on how much better the townhouse looked since the "SPRING CLEANING" had begun. So of course, I couldn't just stop there. I have always been a thinker and I knew that this thought of "SPRING CLEANING" wasn't just heavy on my mind and heart because I had a couple of closets, rooms, and a to-do-list to do...absolutely not! LOL!

I knew that my very own life was going through a much needed "SPRING CLEANING". I had some hidden things, issues of my heart, some overcrowded life closets, some underutilized abilities that had been tucked away too long. I found out that something's in my life weren't finished but just needed some new batteries or needed to be connected to the charger. I found many things that I had been holding on to for too long that I need to get rid of....and as I would step back throughout the process and look at the progress, I noticed that I was on to something.

I realized the more thorough I was the better I felt. So, I ask each of you today...Are you worth doing some "SPRING CLEANING" on? Are you willing to begin and thoroughly deal with different aspects of your life? Will you deal with even the hidden things? Will you stop making excuses, pointing the finger, and remain the victim in your life or will you begin to put in that much needed work? How much better would this world be if we all began to do SPRING CLEANING on our lives? To bring it in even more how much better will your natural home be when you begin to do a real SPRING CLEANING on your life?

I know there are some of you that are perfect and keep an immaculate life but for those of us who are a "WORK IN PROGRESS" I encourage you today to pause and take some time to do some SPRING CLEANING in your life! Begin to touch the areas you have been putting off for years? Get a ladder, get behind some things, and begin to work on YOU! Let US all begin or continue SPRING CLEANING our lives...WE ARE ABSOLUTELY WORTH IT!

Whatever you do, work at it with all your heart, as working for the Lord, not for men- **Colossians 3:2**

Rest

REST...it sounds simple enough right? However, as I have been forced to do it today...so many thoughts are racing through my mind. It literally took me having a 101.3 temp, body aches, and a doctor to tell me you need to REST for me to finally REST! So, as I was laying in my bed thinking about why it wasn't just easy for me to drop everything, pull the covers over my head, and slide into the BEST REST ever. My CONFESSION is that being the oldest child, growing up in a single parent home (for the majority of my childhood), and teaching myself from an early age that I was ALWAYS going to be RESPONSIBLE no matter what has caused me to always GO, Go, GO without always using wisdom on when to REST.

I know I'm not the only person that no matter how you may feel at times you still PRESS. You are always available, usually willing, and oftentimes constantly looking for opportunities to help someone else. Even when you go to REST you think about the clothes that could be washed, a project that needs to be completed, an errand that still needs to be ran, something at work that you need to finish, or a phone call that you meant to make. We make promises to ourselves and even attempt to write REST on our list of things to do...yet, somehow REST keeps getting put on the back burner of our lives. When you add being a mother to that list it becomes even easier to neglect ourselves from the REST we need.

Ironically enough I started team teaching a class entitled "Balancing Life's Demands". When I first was given the book and read the title, I immediately busted out laughing. I knew the God I have learned to love and appreciate so much, indeed has a BIG sense of humor. God has repeatedly put me in positions where as I'm pouring out, I'm also learning and growing. I haven't quite mastered the ability to balance my life's demands but what I am learning to do is to make every adjustment I need to make along the way. I have often taken pride in the fact that I generally am able to get everything done but what I was overlooking was ensuring that I allowed myself to get proper REST! As well as, to ensure that I allowed wisdom to tug at me causing me to learn how to politely say NO and learn to create peaceful times of REST!

So, what I leave with you today is more than a message of REST but a gentle reminder that our bodies are not like shoes, clothes, objects, food, property, or even people that we can easily replace. Our bodies are a ONE TIME ISSUE and it is our personal responsibility to take care of the bodies we have been blessed with. If we neglect to properly take care of our bodies, it affects us more than we can oftentimes see. It's essential that we pause to take a self-evaluation of the excuses we make that block us from properly securing REST for ourselves. If we are not careful, we will develop a habit of neglecting proper REST in our lives and we will begin to accept that as the norm.

Oftentimes many things in our lives have shifted from neglect to the norm as we sacrifice what's best for us. We temporarily make ourselves feel better as we promise once again that we will do better and we will schedule the proper

REST in our lives. However, as the days that turn into years rapidly past, we have not successfully eliminated this pattern of unacceptable norm in our lives. Over time a lot of factors can play into this but we should LOVE ourselves enough to say..."Starting today I am going to make a better effort of taking care of myself!" REST....REST...REST...so when you arise you can be your BEST!

It is God who arms me with strength, and makes my way perfect. –
Psalm 18:32

The Confessions Of Church Girls

The Purpose

Introduce Yourself...Introduce Yourself

"Introduce yourself...introduce yourself.... My name is Marchet....YEA...I'm from Hawaii....YEA...I almost gave up...YEA...but God stepped in on time!"

I'm not sure how many of you remember that cheer or chant! When I was much younger my friends and I would clap our hands and stomp our feet as we DECLARED out loud WHO WE WERE!!! It was almost with little effort that these bold and playful DECLARATIONS would come out! I chuckle even now as I remember one of my childhood originals LOL..."Introduce yourself.... Introduce yourself...My name is Marchet...Yea...I'm CHOCOLATE skinned...YEA...if you don't like me.... YEA...then don't be my friend!" LOL!

We would go on and on for hours taking turns...some were serious but most were graced with humor and ended with tons of laughter! I know we didn't even realize then how POWERFUL it was to stand together and DECLARE out loud who we were and definitely who we were not! Even those who had never done it before or who were generally shy would eventually peel out of their shells and allow their DECLARATIONS to ring!

Today I thought about when and why did we stop doing those DECLARATIONS? Whether we realized it or not those were what I now call "IRON SHARPEN IRON SESSIONS"! These sessions forced us to look at ourselves and CELEBRATE who we were! They forced us to CELEBRATE our strengths! As well as, to CELEBRATE our dreams and to CELEBRATE our goals! It was a hand clapping, foot stomping time of agreement...and if for some reason someone got stuck along the way a FRIEND would chime in and fill in the "blank"!

Everyone usually enjoys a good reason to have a party. I know we have Scentsy, Mary Kay, Artistry, birthday, promotion, jewelry, just because, and why not? parties...but I say we start some "INTRODUCE YOURSELF" parties!!! When is the last time you DECLARED to yourself or a circle of individuals who you really are? When is the last time we've gathered together to ENCOURAGE one another and to ENCOURAGE ourselves?

Right before I was going to reread, finish this chapter, and add my ending I read something written by Deloney McNeary Denson entitled "I AM DYING". It spoke volumes to why I even decided to launch my blog and now this book in the first place! Often, we take RIGHT NOW for granted! If we are not careful, we live a life that believes tomorrow is promised! So, we tend to make a To-Do-List and a Bucket list. If we are not careful, we find ourselves talking about what we are going to do vs. DOING ANYTHING!

I DECLARE its time we REINTRODUCE ourselves because as Deloney so beautifully put "we are dying...we are one day closer to the end of our life here in earth!" It's time we go back to the days where we DECLARED who we are...where we encouraged one another and "filled in the blanks". Open up your mouth, clap your hands, stomp your feet, and shout out your personal declarations! There is so much POWER in our words! The choice is yours if you choose to use your words to give life to yourself and others or to use your words to kill! Whether you kill dreams, motivation, purpose, determination, progress, a consistent stride, or anything else with your words remember that doesn't have to continue. You can choose to declare root failure on the words you have spoken in the past. Then discipline yourself to tend to the potential crops in your life as you strategically fertilize them with words filled with life! Once you grasp the power you possess and the harvest that will surround you it becomes easier to make the necessary shift…REINTRODUCE YOURSELF!

Words kill, words give life; they're either poison or fruit—you choose. -**Proverbs 18:21 MSG**

It Is What It Is!

Have you ever just had a day or week that had you right at the edge? Despite you waking up positive, pouring out, proclaiming it's a NEW day, encouraging others, or moving forward...LIFE has a way of presenting itself to you! In fact, if most people are really honest there are things in this life, we all wish we could change...however, no matter how many times you click your feet, go to bed early thinking tomorrow it will be different, or write down your vision or plan of where you want to be...there are things in life we MUST deal with! It's at those moments that we must firmly proclaim "IT IS WHAT IT IS!!!!"

I personally have experienced what seemed to be an ongoing series of TEST that tried to waiver my faith! Many questions I asked God and many phone calls from those closest to me left me saying, "God, I know you are REAL but how do I/they/we deal with all of this? What do you do at the cemetery of someone you love? How does your mind begin to digest and accept the fact that your child, mother, best friend, or relative is no longer here? Why did they cheat? Why did they walk away? Why was I sexually molested? How come people continue to tear me down instead of building me up? Why are people so jealous, deceitful, & proud to live their lives as an undercover Judas? Why is there so much hate, senseless killings, and a gravitation towards evil? Why is my child, spouse, friend, or family member sick? H ow long will I be here? Why was I raped in college by someone I trusted? When can I get off of this ride? Amongst many other real-life questions.

Yes, I am the author of many blogs and I teach a foundation class at church. Yes, if you call me, I will encourage you, pray for you, and ensure you at least laugh before you hang up the phone. Yet, my CONFESSION is I found when many questions decorated my mind, plus an assortment of things to do almost seemed to be suffocating me, and at those moments where a random tear was rolling down my face...yet I had literally only a "few" I knew I could call!!!

Am I the only one that even though you can call the "few"... sometimes what you are experiencing is so REAL that you just don't call? Most people would not even be able to handle the fact that although "I SMILE" it doesn't mean my heart doesn't hurt or that my life is now free from trials? Oftentimes, we go through such a series of events, disappointments, heart aches, uncertainties, unanswered questions, transitions, and life lessons (at what seems to be a RAPID pace) that our emotions never really catch up!

I've learned through this process that if I need to take things one second at a time IT'S ABSOLUTELY OK!!! I've learned to accept things that I can't change! As well as, to surround myself with people who will serve me the TRUTH in LOVE! I've learned to look at circumstances and issues that use to paralyze me then PROCLAIM "IT IS WHAT IT IS!!"

Let's just pause and be REAL if someone continually chooses to be two-faced and fake, or hurtful, or angry, or stuck, or _____ you fill in the blank...how long are you going to allow it to affect you? If it seems as if your circumstances aren't changing, doors aren't opening, your still carrying CHURCH HURT, you are still in love with someone that is clearly not in love with you, you find yourself repeating the same "woe is me script for your life", or once again _____ you fill in the blank!

When we say "IT IS WHAT IT IS" this is in NO way giving you permission to accept just anything, to lower your standards, or to not apply FAITH! What this chapter is encouraging you to do is to look at your life and all that makes it up...then ACKNOWLEDGE it! ACKNOWLEDGE it without allowing yourself to be bound, depressed, beaten down, or discouraged! It's time that we as CHURCH GIRLS begin living our lives as WARRIORS and not WOUNDED WOMEN!

At some point we have to MOVE FORWARD in ALL AREAS of our lives! This is bigger than what people can see or what we hide behind our beautiful smiles! This means collectively we are going to have to take RESPONSIBILITY for our lives! We have to shift out of park, then neutral, and begin to actively drive forward!

I will end with this thought. I use to work at a school and during one of the class transitions there was a young smiling boy who was approaching me! As he approached there were two words in BOLD PRINT on his t-shirt. His t-shirt read "DOING IT!" I immediately started chuckling that Nike had MOVED FORWARD from "Just Do It" to "DOING IT!" I CONFESS personally and I speak to all of us collectively it's time to shift gears from talking about doing it to actually DOING IT! As we work through our lives and ACKNOWLEDGE things we can say without fear "IT IS WHAT IT IS!" I may not be where I need to be but I'M MOVING FORWARD! I may not have what you or I think I should have but I'M MOVING FORWARD! The sooner we digest "IT IS WHAT IT IS" the sooner we can MOVE FORWARD! CHURCH GIRLS & NON-CHURCH GIRLS may the t-shirts of our lives BOLDLY proclaim that we are DOING IT as we live our BEST lives!

Do you not know that those who run in a race all run, but one receives the prize? Run in such a way that you may obtain it. – **1 Corinthians 9:24**

I've Learned Through This Process

I've learned through this process that if I need to take things one second at a time.... it's ok!!! I've learned to accept things that I can't change and I have learned to say out loud "IT IS WHAT IT IS!" Oftentimes as a CHURCH GIRL I was scared to admit the realities in my life! In my mind I had created these CHURCH GIRL rules that I felt I had to live up to...mostly because I had seen so many other "SAINTS" living that way! You know the ones that act like all is well when really, they are overwhelmed, underappreciated, and unsure of who they really are. The ones who act as if they have never struggled with anything and their flesh has always been under control...lol! The ones that looked at my skirt when it was long and swore, I was "living holy for God" but little did they know it was when my skirt was long (not short) that it was over my head as I laid in the preacher's son's bed.

I've learned that oftentimes people can't handle "IT" so instead of dealing with things head on and declaring "IT IS WHAT IT IS" we join the multitudes of people who rarely give a truthful reply or honest answer. It's so easy if we are not careful to live a life that appears to be one way but in reality, it's another. I guess most Christians justify this behavior by calling it faith. Now don't tilt your church hat and get your slips in a frenzy before hearing me completely out. We are to walk by faith. The bible instructs us "For we walk by faith, not by sight", in 2 Corinthians 5:7. Trust me I'm not saying to not do that. What I am saying is that to never deal with the realities of who we really are cannot be hidden behind the comforts of 2 Corinthian 5:7. We must get to a point that yes; we are believing that this area in our life will be different. However, RIGHT NOW we must put in work on our end to make the necessary changes. Our church attire, church titles, church position, church volunteer work, church attendance, and church _____ cannot camouflage the realities of our life forever. You can have all the church _____ checked off and still be living outside of reality.

We have to give ourselves and each other the permission to be authentic. To share amongst each other the process it took for us to get where we are. How soon we forget and dismiss the grace and love of God that has cocooned our life. Sometimes it's helpful to take off the church hats, to be without a title or position for a moment, to get poured into instead of always pouring out, to let your relationship with God be your motivation vs. church attendance and a gold star. Be FREE so other women and girls can be FREE as well. Our report card is the fruit we see right within our own churches. It's time to ask ourselves the hard questions. Where are the young girls that were raised in church? Why are so many of them running to clubs and tattoo bars before they desire to run to church? Why is depression, suicide, low self-esteem, low body image, and a decrease of attending church so high within our churches? The questions are endless but if we don't start being real and addressing these issues, we will continue to have services with spiritually fat people. While the ones that truly need the Word are outside the church walls. It's time to stop letting our church girls get lost in the process and begin to ask ourselves the hard question...what are YOU going to do about it?

The name of the LORD is a strong tower; the righteous run to it and are safe. – **Proverbs 18:10**

Lately

Lately....I have had a lot of time to step back and reflect on life. This life I have lived as a "church girl"...this life I have lived in general has been full of twist and turns. The more I live the more I realize that I can't live this life without God. For periods in my life, I tried. I tried to do it based on how I felt or what I was trying to not face but every single time it led me right back to God.

I tried to fill my life with people. The reality is you can't live this life without encountering people. If we are not careful people will begin to steer our lives in directions that it was never intended to go. WE have to be very careful who we connect with...who we "LATELY" have allowed to enter the intimate corridors of our lives. Too often we take the interactions we have with others too lightly. We often say

"Oh _____ she/he is my friend...or _____ I've known them my whole life...or _____ they got my back...until we get to LATELY!

My Granny use to say "Marsha...live a little and you will see." Throughout the years that hasn't struck the core of me until LATELY! I'm accepting the realities of this life we live. I'm accepting the fact that my LATELY is filled with mirrors that are making me look at ME and look at what is really going on. I'm realizing that this life we live is bigger than twist and turns but is intended for us to reach our full potential with God.

I use to think that loving God was such a sacrifice. I had allowed so many untruths to penetrate my mind that I almost missed the ultimate sacrifice. LATELY God has been dealing with me about ME! LATELY my outlook is changing...my need to fill my life with people is changing....my need to always be on the go...my need to be in control! (I realize all these examples start with "MY NEED") LATELY I've had to step back and look at 40 plus years of life and ask myself some hard questions. I had to confront some things about myself that weren't always easy to digest. I had to ask myself do you want to keep duplicating nonsense or do you want to discipline yourself to reach your full potential?

I don't know what your LATELY has been but LATELY I'm realizing that it's time to fill my life with some new things. It's time to start my days different. It's time to live INTENTIONALLY and LATELY is exactly where I'm supposed to be! It's never too late to regroup and it's never too late to (church girl or not) surrender your life to God. Keep Smiling and if you don't remember anything else remember God loves YOU no matter where you are LATELY!

But seek first his kingdom and his righteousness, and all these things will be given to you as well. – **Matthew 6:33**

The Confessions Of Church Girls

Loving Yourself

Reflecting on this thing we call LIFE...I'm amazed that my tear ducts can still formulate tears...that my body yet feels emotions...and that I am still standing! I've learned in this life that we all have our own journeys we must take. For you to compare yours to mine...devalues...the true essence of your life. For each experience is unique in itself. Each journey has its own set of definitions, boundaries, sorrows, and triumphs. This life we must live will slip swiftly past you if you are not careful. As you fixate your eyes on such irrelevant circumstance's life is ticking away. Daily my goal is to make this day better than the day before. For years I've been on the same roller coaster ride. When the opportunity to get off that ride and get on a more enjoyable one would present itself. I stayed right where I was. Why? Why did I allow myself to revisit the same things over and over again? Why didn't I realize the power within me to change the course of my life? Why did it take so long? The answer is so simple...it's because I didn't truly love myself.

If I could teach a class on anything it would be on LOVING YOURSELF. In loving yourself you can better love others. You will never truly know the essence of love until you have a love relationship with yourself. Oftentimes it's our past. Past circumstances, past trials, past hurts, past fears, past relationships, past friendships, past disappointments...I think you get the point...OUR PAST...can hold our future captive. It is not until we deal with our past that we can really steadily move through our present! That has become one of my goals. As I get older my goal in life is to finally get off that roller coaster and to experience the many experiences that my life is intended to bring.

You have to stop yourself from just focusing on the negative and to really take a look at how BLESSED you really are. As I type this out even now, I had to chuckle within myself on how long I have actually allowed this roller coaster to continue. I mean I am the amusement park queen. I look forward to a good roller coaster but wouldn't a roller coaster loose it's zing if you just stayed on it for years. Not only would you eventually literally get sick of it but you have also prevented yourself from seeing all the other attractions within the amusement park. That is far from a deep analogy but the reality of the message has evident roots in many of our lives.

It's time to pull this thing up by the root! We could compare stories all day long... about who had it the worst...what we had to go through...etc., etc., etc....OR instead we could reflect on what's real. Acknowledging and accepting the fact that this life we are living is but a vapor! You have to work this life out and daily wake up knowing this might be your last day. It is time to do it! Believe me when I say I'm often times typing to myself and you all are just reading my personal conversation...LOL. It is time for me, you, US...to live today and realize the strength we possess. If you can't seem to do it for yourself right now just begin to digest the fact that someone needs, you to get your life together! (SMILE)

As I look at the people that God has allowed my paths to cross with, I realize that this life is so much bigger than what my mind can fathom. Oftentimes it's your ability to master self-love that will move you right into your real destiny. I believe this life is not about just you. That it goes beyond you. I believe that each of us once we daily work on self-love...will see what God really intended that we need to sow into each other! That's where you are weak, I am strong and where I am weak you are strong! There is so much power in unity and coming together!

This brings my mind to the saying that sometimes people are like crabs. Once they see one crab trying to get out of the pot...they do everything in their power to pull that crab down. The key to this life is to learn to flip it. To be the type of person that lives a life that is beyond themselves. Instead of pulling someone else down, hating, or comparing you should be the type of individual that is going to help others reach their full potential. It's vital as individuals and collectively that we really catch on to that. There is so much that lies <u>within you</u> that is not just intended for you!!! What makes up you can be the very thing that will encourage the next person, give them hope, or open doors that would otherwise be closed!

It's the simple things that cause us to stumble and miss the big picture. Yes, we are human but we have lost the wisdom our ancestors had. It was the wisdom that they shared amongst themselves to get each other out of a bounding situation. That wisdom opened the flood gates of freedom for so many others in a time when their lives, their masters, and everything around them was trying to YELL out that they were nothing! They had no choice but to develop a SELF LOVE. They had to learn to LOVE THEMSELVES and to not allow their eyes to preoccupy on what seemed more than obvious.

Just imagine for a second the conditions they lived in and the discipline it took to develop enough faith to look beyond their present situation. They had to learn that in spite of what others thought, what others did to them, what they felt, and what it looked like that they were incredible individuals that were destined for greatness. It took one person making a decision to LOVE THEMSELVES that had a rippling effect on others. Can you imagine the power of one person that makes a decision and then they turn around and share that decision with someone else? We can't just look at where we are now as a people, we need to stay focused on our goals and start making better decisions!

I confess, that this is an area that I'm aggressively working on! I know that within me lies too much to stay on pause forever! I now challenge myself and you to reexamine ourselves and to no longer take for granted even a second of life! LOVE is the key! LOVE YOURSELF because you were uniquely made for such a time as this! SEIZE IT…YOU ARE WORTH IT!

And now these three remain: faith, hope and love. But the greatest of these is love. -**1 Corinthians 13:13 NIV**

Purpose

I woke up this morning and went on Facebook. It's one of the things I do every day because I feel like Facebook is my bridge to my family and friends who are not in Italy with me. So, as I was updating my status, checking my notifications, and scrolling down I see the below:

"To Marchet and all who need this: You are on the path you are on for a purpose. So, before you question or curse the boulder in your path or the one who put it there, keep in mind that what lies beneath it could quite possibly change your life."

I paused for a minute scrolled back up and then scrolled back down for a minute thinking that what my eyes had just read was attributed to me being a little sleepy…lol. So, as I scrolled back down it was still there. With my name right after "To". It was like Fran knew or better yet God knew that at that very moment I needed some clarity and encouragement on this "BOULDER" of an experience I was going through. What started off as what I thought to be the beginning of new things seemed to drastically turn into a rapid, heart breaking, lonely walk through the pits of hell. I've picked up the phone many times during this ordeal. Oftentimes in anger doing what my mind said should be done. Hell, he had hurt me and I felt like I should run but somehow my feet stayed on this foreign soil.

The more I tried to do what seemed like the 100% answer to this whole large adulterous dose of pain I found myself "STILL". Still here, still hurting, and still unsure how this all calculated to me being so called "BLESSED." I tried not to be angry with God, with Pastor, with every person that had ever paused to encourage me or to give me what God told them "Italy" was going to be for me. From "the moment your feet touch the ground you are going to be blessed" to "God is going to save and do a work in your husband and your family," "this time will be a time for just you, your husband, and the girls…watch how God proves himself to you."

Honestly, all those words when I was in Italy seemed like

Castor oil that I had to slowly and often times daily digest. I had to let the words settle within my mind and soul. Naturally you would think the woman that taught the young people the Word of God, allowed God to use her, and often had a word of encouragement for everyone else could surely encourage herself. "Come on Marchet, quote those scriptures, pray those mountain moving prayers you prayed, cast the devil out, put holy oil all over the walls of your home, and anoint your home so that the devil could have no place. For this is holy ground" Yet, I found myself sinking into a pity party full of unanswered questions, few scriptures, minimal prayer (usually only for my food), and the only oil was in my hair or the olive oil I used to create a meal.

It should be as easy as pumping a tire up. God is the source…I need some air (some lifting), insert some God in you Chet, and get pumped up! Yet, I was deteriorating and sinking into the grip of anger, disappointment, resentment, and fatigue. I was becoming a prisoner to a situation and to a battle that this Christian soldier didn't want to fight. I had predetermined in my mind that I had fought in the classrooms of 208, 206, and 204. Doesn't that give me a Hall Pass from warfare for at least 3 years? Hey God, I'll even settle for 1 year. I forgot that I had to keep my war clothes on I thought I could replace them with a pink and black lingerie and a bag full of sexual tricks. Nope for some reason I have a different route. This God I served wanted more of me. I couldn't figure out how much more was left. What do you want from me God? Did I piss you off somewhere along the way and now I'm still paying for it? I couldn't see this thing consistently in the right way.

All I could see was the pain I was feeling. All I could see was that I had been fighting for so long that surely there was another Christian that could tag in for 3 years. Why couldn't I just have a happy marriage? Why can't I be normal? How long Lord and Why me? The more I pondered the more I realized that not only did I have all these dogs on questions but I was ALONE! God, do you realize I am in Italy? Do you realize that I have no car? No job? No Mama? No ACE BOON COONS? No FAITHFUL few? No shoulder to cry on? No church? (Not that I really wanted a church because now I was at the point that I just wanted to have someone on one time with God!!!) Yes, God!

Remember me God? Remember me? How in the world do I feel so far away from you? Why do the same scriptures that use to excite me feel like weights? Why do you have me here in the middle of what feels like an unsolvable Rubik's Cube challenge? Is the joke on me God? Am I the sacrificial lamb? Am I the brunt of the joke? Did I ask you already God if I pissed you off?

No, I'm here for a PURPOSE!!!! A PURPOSE!!!! As I lift this "boulder" up as often as I can to try to see the light and to inhale some hope of a brighter day. A PURPOSE!!! This has changed my life already. I feel as if I'm in a car…better yet a BIG Red Hummer. The seat belt has been strapped on me and my hands aren't even on the wheel. I'm on God's cruise control. I hear Shelia's voice telling me "Marchet, pass the test." For this test as much as I would love to have Shelia come take it for me is the REAL DEAL. This is hands on experience where I see what I'm really made out of. Where I see will these bones live? Is God a man that He should lie? Where I step back and deal with what has been really dealing with me. Shelia dropped something on me a couple of days ago that it's not about the "other woman!" I then grasped that it's really not about my ex-husband either. It's about me. It's about me going all the way through this COMPLETELY trusting God and truthfully saying "God, I can't see all of this yet....and I have never quite felt like this before. I feel so vulnerable, so open, so naked, so on a bungee jump of my life that it makes me uncomfortable. I like being in control God. I like planning and knowing what's next. I guess I have to accept the fact that in this part of my life you are keeping a close hand. The only way I can see your hand is to come closer to you and to spend more time with you. I no longer have the substitute of teaching the 7th-Young Adults class, attending church, or retreating face to face with the faithful few. This leg of this race is a one-on-one personal training hour with you."

You would think this church girl would be confident in resting completely in You. Yet, I find that I haven't "rested" in a long time. I find that as I tuck the Super Woman suit into the purple suitcase, I brought to Italy that there is a woman who needs you to do a work in her. There is a woman that needs you to touch her where human hands can't touch! I need you God to go beyond my church girl experience and touch my life with your real love, your guidance, your will.

I realize this phase requires a complete surrender. A backwards fall into your hands COMPLETELY TRUSTING THAT YOU GOT ME! You got me God, right? I guess I have to come closer and closer to really get the answers. So, I'm walking God…here I come…please don't disappoint me like every man in my life has. This is about healing. I lay on your surgical table and I ask you Lord to go to the places that many don't know about. Go to the hurt. Go to the deceit. Go to the hidden places. Go to the childhood hurts. Go to the religious cover-ups. God Go!!! Go God because I can't carry this BOULDER and I can't remove this, remove that, remove it all…without YOU!

I NEED YOU GOD! SINCERELY,

A WOUNDED CHURCH GIRL

And my God will supply all your needs according to His riches in glory in Christ Jesus. – **Philippians 4:19**

Marchet

Often times as I begin to write I think about how long I've vividly seen this part of my life! I have always been someone that worked through the various happenings of my life through engaging with a pen and paper or now engaging with my iPhone or laptop! As long as I can remember I have been someone that expresses herself through writing. When I was younger it was my escape from reality. I could write and say how I really felt like a cup filled to the rim that needs to release what was within.

Working on this book, that was originally a blog, has taught me a lot about myself. As I was rereading some of the things I wrote, over these past years, I almost had forgotten the intensity of some of the events. It wasn't that I didn't live it but for the majority of my life I have learned that I suppress things in order to cope. It started when I was a little girl and I couldn't understand why I didn't have a daddy at home? Or why my last name was different than all my brothers and sisters? As I look back at an early age, I had to grow up in a sense to cope with the things in my life. I struggled with low self-esteem and other people made me hate being dark skinned. I remember being in the tub wishing I could rub all the dark skin off of me because more people teased me about it vs. those who celebrated my dark skin.

I remember at an early age just thinking I wasn't enough. In my little head it started with not having a father around. I didn't know what it felt like to call a man Daddy until I was around 10 years old and I finally met my biological father for the first time. I remember it was at a Holiday Inn. My mom drove up to the hotel and my dad was there. I was going to spend the summer with him and in the back seat was my sister Vellice and my brother Ronnie was shotgun. I remember as we drove from the hotel, I whispered to my sister Vellice, "What should I call him?" In true Vellice style she said, "Daddy silly!" LOL! As simple as that sounds it was the first of many awkward encounters with men in my life. I always second guessed my stance with them or my true value.

Fast forward to today, July of 2016, I'm literally 6 months' post-divorce. Looking back, I thought the lies and the adultery were the hardest part of my story. However, to my surprise the actual divorce process trumped the lies and adultery. The hardest part about going through the divorce is because it's actually feels like you are going through a real death. Over the past couple of years, I have experienced the heart wrenching pain of losing several important people in my life. It wasn't that I didn't know that the reality of death was real. I just never had to experience the realness of death as close and as often as I have over the past 5 years or so. When my step dad died, I never would have thought that my husband wouldn't have been by my side. He couldn't be my side because he was completely trying to be apart from me. It made the divorce that much harder because I felt as if everything was dying around me at the same time. I never would have imagined that he wouldn't be there. The reality of the matter was that he wasn't so that added to an already hurtful situation.

Instead of this process being one that my husband would be looking out for the best interest of our girls. He lied and hustled his way to only have to pay $200 total a month for both of our daughters. How does someone say they love their children with one breath but yet thinks $25 a week is sufficient to raise them? Though he may send additional funds he refuses to produce his pay stubs so the child support can legally be adjusted. That just doesn't add up but in the math book of my ex-husband that would have to be sufficient and that obviously seemed like the right thing to do. It's amazing how the truth finds a way of coming out and the same man that swore he had no job and was living with his Mama. Really was living with the woman he committed adultery with and only wanted to rush the divorce because she was pregnant that year. I guess miracles do happen when a child can still be born after a successful vasectomy or karma just found a way to reveal the realities of who he chose to sacrifice his family for. He obviously wasn't the only one that her legs were spreading eagle for. All I can say is may they continue to have an open and truth filled relationship.

Some may ask why are you putting it all out there? My simple answer would be because it's the graphic truth. I've carried the guilt of feeling as if there was something I could have done to change the circumstances. What I've learned is our issues were deeper than an orgasm on the side. The root of the matter is that this CHURCH GIRL decided to link herself up with a man that was incapable of telling the truth. I remember the first time we went to the bay area to see where his grandparents lived, to meet his dad, his aunt, his cousins, and to spend time at his mom's house. I was casually talking to his mom and talking about how the girls were Puerto Rican and Black (side note because my ex-husband had told me early on when we were dating that he was Puerto Rican and Black). His mom paused and looked at me as if I said something she had heard before. She went on to tell me he has being saying that lie since he was a little boy.

He's Greek and Black...and not Puerto Rican. Now you have to understand that I was shocked because the girls weren't babies anymore and their entire life, we had been telling them they were Puerto Rican and Black. I even was telling other people because they would naturally ask since I was obviously dark skinned and both the girls had light skin. I had no reason at all to think the man that I exchanged vows with would lie about his ethnicity...yet he did! It's another example of if we don't deal with something early on in our lives it will pour into our lives later.

I didn't pick that up when we were dating that here is a man that will lie about anything. The only reason I was really mad at his side chic is because she openly admitted with a big dose of sarcasm that she was aware he had a wife and two daughters. Yet, she basically didn't care! I know everyone says you should be mad at the man because he's the one that was in a covenant marriage with you and not her. The truth of the matter is I don't blame her for the adultery. I blame her for being the type of woman that didn't have enough self-control and self-esteem to wait to spread her legs like an eagle until he was divorced. Now almost 6 years or so later my anger has transitioned into gratitude because he is now her problem and she is his problem!

However, I must CONFESS that didn't happen overnight. I didn't have this sense of "Grace and Peace" be upon you both until I realized they were draining my life! I look back and realize man Marchet you were fighting for a man that couldn't have loved you. You were fighting for a man that doesn't really care about the best interest of his daughters. You were fighting for a man that when he could of chose you, he chose her and 2 other women before that. You were fighting for a man that was lying to you and lying to them. You were fighting for a man that knew your dad just died and didn't care. You were fighting for a man that literally hates you because love doesn't act like that. So whatcha gonna do Marchet? GET NAKED was my answer! This time around I wasn't talking about getting naked for the intent to get in the bed. This time it meant stripping the realities of my life to the core so I could finally deal with it. This is what The

Confessions of Church Girls is all about. It's about sharing your truth so someone else will not have to experience the pit falls and valleys attached to your choices.

Don't get me wrong. I'm not this angry black woman typing this book and not acknowledging that I had any faults. I did. My first mistake was allowing myself to get connected with someone who didn't share my same beliefs. I pulled my panties down faster than I should of and the effort I used to be intimate with him should have been the effort I used to really find out who he was!

I just wanted to be loved and my entire life that has been the ongoing truth. I so desperately wanted to be a wife and to have the family I didn't see for the majority of my childhood. So, without really knowing it I just accepted whatever. It didn't just start with my ex-husband either. I had this desire to just please that started from when I was a child. I would get so nervous around my biological father that I would say "axes" instead of "ask." It would drive the very core of the college professor that my dad was crazy. He would yell…it's "Ask not axes." It's funny now but I remember as a child I was so nervous that I couldn't get it right. I would keep saying "Axes" and he would keep yelling "Asks." I would never speak up and say, "I know but right now I'm just not getting it because you are making me nervous." I kept that pattern of not speaking up in all of my relationships with men. For those that know me that may seem hard to believe but the truth is I'm vocal in other areas of my life but with men I shut down. I become the pleaser. If they need something I will go over and beyond to get it. Yet, rarely I wouldn't do the same for myself. It's a harsh truth to digest but I've finally accepted that it is indeed reality.

I remember I was dating this guy from New Orleans who also was a liar. Lord, as I'm typing this chapter about me, I'm really seeing the patterns in my life. This CHURCH GIRL left the TRUTH of God and consistently got attached to LIARS. Anyways, this guy wanted to start this magazine. I would stay up late and wake up early to research and find out information. While at the same time I always wanted to write books myself. I put hours and hours into fueling his dream.

I even made a mock up magazine that featured me on the cover (LOL of course) because I really wanted him to fulfill his dreams. Then it came out after I was "Bonnie" (that ride or die chic) and stayed with him during his federal prison stint that…Oh I'm not the only "Bonnie" in your life and you chose the "Bonnie" with the hair net on her head to be your wife! Oh…ooookkkkk! Another CHURCH GIRL epic fail!

When I look back on that relationship as a whole and the other relationships, I was in I realize that my decisions were horrible. I was so tunnel vision and so caught up in how fine this one was or that one was that I continued to make bad choices and compromised the very essence of who I was intended to be. Most CHURCH GIRLS never want to admit that or want to regroup. I had to accept the fact that I was attracting LIARS because I was an easy prey. I was so anxious to be loved that I became an easy target. There was no chase to get me. You just had to me fine, funny, and talk to me. I shake my head as I realize how innocently desperate, I really was. It's a humbling situation when you have to come back to your roots and admit you pulled away.

So where do we go from here? How do you regroup as a CHURCH GIRL and get yourself back on track? The answer to those questions for me was I had to deal with the lies and start digesting the truth again. The first lie I had to deal with is the negative spin the enemy tried to plant in my head concerning the very words "CHURCH GIRL." For so long I've almost felt like being a CHURCH GIRL was a bad thing! In my head it meant restricted, boxed in, different, and a bunch of rules. When in reality it meant highly favored, set apart, destined for greatness, prayed for, and full of purpose. How drastic were the seeds and lies that have been planted in my head since a child? It's the enemies' job to try to make us CHURCH GIRLS begin to believe the lies!

If you think church is boring and that there isn't nothing going on inside the church walls. You will plot and run, as soon as you get a chance, as far away from church and God as you can! How do I know this because I lived it? I remember when I first came to University of Hawaii for college. I had packed all my Jesus posters for my dorm room walls and I had my bible in tow. I really loved God and at that time I was just excited to be going to college. So eventually I became a Resident Advisor. This allowed me to have my very own room and bathroom in one of the four circle dorms. I was so excited and still focused. So little did I know that word started getting around campus that I was a "CHURCH GIRL." So don't try to date "her" because she loves Jesus.

Anyway, later in the semester this basketball player approaches me and says, "Hey I heard you love Jesus and I was wondering if you wanted to have Bible Study some time?" So, I was thinking, "Yippee someone wants to learn about the Lord and they actually aren't asking me to go to a party again?" LOL! It's funny now as I'm typing and reading this but those are my real-life scenarios.

So, me and this basketball player started having bible studies. The first and I believe the second time were focused bible studies. Then this CHURCH GIRL got caught up and the bible study became second priority. He was saying all the right things and had this incredible wit about him. It was like one minute we were talking about the book of John and the next minute we were talking about how pretty my chocolate skin was. Now remember that was big time for me. Especially, since I struggled loving my chocolate skin for years. I literally avoided sun contact, never like going to the beach or an outdoor pool (even though I was raised in Hawaii), and saw myself as literally less than.

Now just imagine being someone who for years had low self-esteem about her chocolate skin and now this 6'3" basketball player from California was telling me how great my chocolate skin was. The more he talked the less I cared about John, Timothy, or even Matthew. Sadly, I was like an inflated balloon that with each compliment or witty comment I was being filled. Before I knew it, I was high and basking in his words because I was not use to hearing them.

I without really recognizing it began to take off my full armor. We went from bible studies, to meeting on campus, to eating dinner together in the cafeteria. Gradually my breast plate of righteousness, my shield of faith, my helmet of salvation, my sword of the spirit, my shoes to spread the gospel of peace, and my belt of truth was coming off quicker than a stripper in Vegas. This CHURCH GIRL was quickly losing focus and as my armor was coming off so was my desire to remain holy. I remember thinking in my mind if this fine basketball player just touches the hem of my shorts, it's on and popping in this dorm room.

That's why we have to be careful what we allow to penetrate the corridors of our mind and to be rehearsed through our lips. He began not only touching the hem of my shorts but the button to my shirt and the notches on my bra. Before I knew it, I wasn't quoting scriptures but now was calling his name and I'm not talking about the name of Jesus either. This was the first time that as a CHURCH GIRL I was engaging in sex without the fear of the preacher and his wife coming through the bedroom door. I had never experienced this before because it wasn't a sneak of passion but a full-on sexual experience and my mind just couldn't catch up. When it was all said and done the same wonderful basketball player who covered me with compliments and ensured that I was pleasured. Had now stood up and gotten dressed. I have not forgotten after almost twenty plus years the last words he left me with. He looked me in my eyes and pointed towards all the Jesus posters I had plastered on my dorm room walls and said…" Shaker you might want to take all those Jesus posters down now!" It was like a brick of reality hit me across my head as the pleasure I just experienced immediately left me. I knew right in that moment that this CHURCH GIRL had indeed messed up!

Isn't that what it's all about. People, including the enemy, knows the real treasure of being a CHURCH GIRL! It is his desire to break us down and for us to start digesting the lies. What I know for sure almost twenty plus years later is I would never trade my full armor again for moments of pleasure. I have tried for a long time now to prove that what the Bible, what the church, and all the saints were trying to tell me was in some way false. The reality of the matter is although the church and the saints weren't perfect people the Bible is a perfect tool to direct our lives. I know everyone won't agree with that and for my nON-CHURCH GIRL friends that's probably when they will throw this book or Kindle version straight across the room.

It is easier to put the blame on everyone else when it comes to why we are or are not doing what we need to do? After you live awhile you realize even the people that were cheering you on to do this or to do that may no longer be around. There comes a time(s) in each of our lives when we begin to deal with what's really dealing with us. When we take the telescope off of church, church people, others, this, or that and we adjust the telescope lens on our own life. I could go on and on with forty plus years of stories but then we wouldn't have anything left for the rest of the books that I'll be writing. So, I will end with this. One of the most beautiful things that a CHURCH GIRL can do is to accept who she is fully and to trust God long enough for him to show you who he really is! Once we stop going through the cycles and stop fighting against God's plan, we will find a peace that passes all understanding. My prayer is that at least one life is changed by reading this. I pray you find the strength to begin to deal with what really is dealing with you and the courage to authentically be who you really are! Just know I may never know your name, our paths may never cross, but I will continually be praying that you "get it" a lot sooner than I did. I will be praying that you learn to embrace being a CHURCH GIRL with pride and for those of you who just aren't interested that you will continue to put the telescope on your life and figure out why not?

Thank you for taking the time to read through various parts of my life and I look forward for our paths crossing again in the pages of my next book!

I love you BIG,

Marchet

aka CHURCH GIRL

God is not a man, that he should lie; neither the son of man, that he should repent: hath he said, and shall he not do it? or hath he spoken, and shall he not make it good? -**Numbers 23:19**

Marchet Denise Fullum

ABOUT THE AUTHOR

Marchet Denise Fullum is a tropical church girl that was raised in Mililani, Hawaii. Her life was forever changed at the age of 10 when she came to the City of Refuge Christian Church. Dr. Wayne E. Anderson poured into her life and spoke prophetically…breaking generational curses and consistently reminded her that she had a right to be free! 97% of the time you will find her smiling or laughing. She is the proud mother of Jayda Louise and Anzel Marchét. Both of her daughters have added additional purpose and motivation to her life. Marchet has her MBA and her Bachelor of Science degree in Fashion Merchandising and Design. She enjoys consulting businesses and doing interior design. Writing has always been an important part of her life from a young age. Her blog and this book "Confessions of Church Girls" were manifested by her genuine love for people, her desire to be a transparent motivation, and her desire to reach those inside and outside the church walls. What she knows for sure is something wonderful happens when individuals free themselves from the secrets, lies, hurts, lessons, and cycles of the past and begin to live their lives to the fullest. God loves big, He has a plan, and He does not lie! So, she has decided to live her best life and to keep smiling through each season of her life!

Made in the USA
Columbia, SC
14 January 2023